Collins gem

TURKISH
PHRASEBOOK
& DICTIONARY

Published by Collins
An imprint of HarperCollins Publishers
Westerhill Road
Bishopbriggs
Glasgow G64 2QT

HarperCollins Publishers
Macken House, 39/40 Mayor Street Upper,
Dublin 1, D01 C9W8, Ireland

Fourth Edition 2016

10 9 8 7 6

© HarperCollins Publishers 1993, 2007,
2010, 2016

ISBN 978-0-00-813595-9

Collins® and Collins Gem® are registered
trademarks of HarperCollins Publishers
Limited

www.collinsdictionary.com

Typeset by Davidson Publishing Solutions

Printed in India

A catalogue record for this book is available
from the British Library.

If you would like to comment on any aspect
of this book, please contact us at the given
address or online.
E-mail: dictionaries@harpercollins.co.uk
 facebook.com/collinsdictionary
 @collinsdict

Acknowledgements
We would like to thank those authors and
publishers who kindly gave permission for
copyright material to be used in the Collins
Corpus. We would also like to thank Times
Newspapers Ltd for providing valuable data.

Editor
Holly Tarbet

Contributors
Ayca Rodop
Gül Ülgen Greenslade
David White

For the Publisher
Gerry Breslin
Janice McNeillie
Helen Newstead

Front cover image:
The Blue Mosque of Istanbul.
©Vincent St. Thomas / Shutterstock.com

Using your phrasebook

Whether you're on holiday or on business, your **Collins Gem Phrasebook and Dictionary** is designed to help you locate the exact phrase you need, when you need it. You'll also gain the confidence to go beyond what is in the book, as you can adapt the phrases by using the dictionary section to substitute your own words.

The **Gem Phrasebook and Dictionary** includes:
- Over 60 topics arranged thematically, so that you can easily find an expression to suit the situation

- Simple pronunciation which accompanies each word and phrase, to make sure you are understood when speaking aloud

- Tips to safeguard against any cultural faux pas, providing the essential dos and don'ts of local customs or etiquette

- A basic grammar section which will help you to build on your phrases

- **FACE TO FACE** dialogue sections to give you a flavour of what to expect from a real conversation

- A handy map of the country which shows the major cities and how to pronounce them

- **YOU MAY HEAR** sections for common announcements and messages, so that you don't miss important information when out and about

- A user-friendly 3000 word dictionary to ensure you'll never be stuck for something to say

- **LIFELINE** phrases are listed on the inside covers for quick reference. These basic words and phrases will be essential to your time abroad

Before you jet off, it's worth spending time looking through the topics to see what is covered and becoming familiar with pronunciation.

The colour key below shows you how to search the phrasebook by theme, so you'll be able to find relevant phrases very quickly.

Talking to people

Getting around

Staying somewhere

Shopping

Leisure

Communications

Practicalities

Health

Eating out

Menu reader

Reference

Grammar

Dictionary

Contents

Pronouncing Turkish

· ·

Turkish uses the same script as English, with one or two unfamiliar letters. Generally it is straightforward to pronounce. You read the words as they are spelled. Pronounce every single letter in the word.

The following letters sound roughly the same as in English: **b d f g h k l m n p r s t** and **z** but note that **r** is always rolled and always pronounced, as in Italian or Russian, and **h** is always a sound in its own right, e.g. **mithat** (meet-hat, not mee-that). In the pronunciation guide we use hyphens for clarity. Where double letters occur, both letters are pronounced, e.g. **dikkat** (deek-kat, not dee-kat), **piller** (peel-ler, not pee-ler).

Letters to watch		Represented by
a	pronounced as in car (never came or have)	a
e	pronounced as in pet (never Pete)	e
i	pronounced as in litre (never light)	ee
o	pronounced as in not (never note)	o
u	pronounced as in blue (never but or cute)	oo
c	pronounced like 'j' in jam (never cap or pace)	dj
g	pronounced as in lag (never large)	g
j	pronounced like the 's' in pleasure (never jam)	zh

7

Letters to watch		Represented by
r	always pronounce the letter 'r' even when it is at the end of the word.	r
s	pronounced as in sag (never basil)	s

Unfamiliar letters		Pronunciation
ı	pronounced like the second 'e' in letter, speaker	uh
ö	pronounced like the 'i' in bird, dirt	ur
ü	pronounced like the 'u' in German Lübeck, French musée, English nude and Tewkesbury	ew
ç	pronounced 'ch' as in chop, church	ch
ş	pronounced 'sh' as in shop, sheep, ship	sh
ğ	silent g: has no sound, but doubles the length of the previous vowel	

Stress

The stress is generally on the last syllable of the word, especially the question suffix at the end of the sentence.

Top ten tips

• •

1 When you visit a Turkish house, the host will say '**Hoşgeldiniz!**' (welcome). You should reply, '**Hoşbulduk**'.

2 Turks are naturally inquisitive about visitors to their country and are keen to hear your impressions of Turkey. Shortly after meeting, you may be asked where you are from, as well as more personal questions about your family life. They may also invite you for further discussion over tea or Turkish coffee.

3 It is totally normal for women or men to kiss each other on the cheeks and hug. It is also normal for people to walk arm in arm or with their arm around someone, regardless of gender. It is a natural expression of affection, along with often touching a person's hand or shoulder during a conversation.

4 Turkish people do not tend to share the bill in restaurants; the person who has extended the invitation will pay. It is polite to offer to share but you shouldn't insist.

5 When drinking Turkish coffee, never drink to the bottom of the cup. It's ground coffee which leaves a thick sediment, like non-filtered espresso! It's a popular superstition to read your fortune in the

shapes created by the coffee dregs – simply turn your coffee cup upside-down onto the plate when you're finished, swirl it, and leave it to dry.

6 When greeting people, shake the hands of the eldest person first. You will also see younger people kiss an older person's right hand and then put it on their forehead. If you are the eldest in the group, be prepared for this, especially from the kids!

7 Shoes are removed when entering someone's home. You shouldn't point the sole of your foot towards anyone, especially an older person, as this can be considered disrespectful.

8 Turks love talking about current affairs, but approach religious and other sensitive political matters with caution – there may often be strong viewpoints on both sides of the debate.

9 If you are invited to somebody's home, it is polite to take a small gift such as a dessert, especially if you are invited for dinner.

10 While in the company of Turkish people, if you are snacking on something (such as a bag of crisps or a packet of biscuits) it is very rude not to offer some to the people around you. If you are not going to offer it to others, do not eat it in front of them! It is also courteous to refrain from eating and drinking in public in fasting hours during Ramadan.

Talking to people

Hello/goodbye, yes/no

Watch out for some confusing body language.
In Turkey shaking your head means 'I don't
understand', not 'no'. A Turkish person indicates
'no' by tilting their head up and back, and raising
their eyebrows. This may be accompanied by a click
of the tongue. 'Yes' is a forward nod of the head.

Please	**Lütfen** lewt-fen	
Thank you	**Teşekkür ederim** te-shek-kewr e-de-reem	
Thanks	**Teşekkürler** te-shek-kewr-ler	
Yes	**Evet** e-vet	
No	**Hayır** ha-yuhr	
Sorry!	**Pardon!** par-don!	
You're welcome	**Rica ederim** ree-dja eh-de-reem	

OK	**Tamam**	
	ta-mam	
Excuse me!	**Afedersiniz!**	
	a-fe-der-see-neez!	
Hello/Hi	**Merhaba/Selam**	
	mer-ha-ba/se-lam	
Goodbye	**Hoşçakal** (if leaving)/	
	Güle güle (if staying behind)	
	hosh-cha-kal/gew-le-gew-le	
Good morning	**Günaydın**	
	gew-nay-duhn	
Good afternoon	**Tünaydın**	
	tew-nay-duhn	
Good day	**İyi günler**	
	ee-yee gewn-ler	
Good evening	**İyi akşamlar**	
	ee-yee ak-sham-lar	
Goodnight	**İyi geceler**	
	ee-yee ge-dje-ler	
I don't understand	**Anlamıyorum**	
	an-la-muh-yo-room	
I don't speak Turkish	**Türkçe bilmiyorum**	
	tewrk-che beel-mee-yo-room	

Key phrases

• •

Is there...?/ Are there...?/ Do you have...?	**...var mı?** ...var muh?
Do you have bread?	**Ekmek var mı?** ek-mek var muh?
Do you have beer?	**Bira var mı?** bee-ra var muh?
Do you have stamps?	**Pul var mı?** pool var muh?
I want/need...	**...istiyorum** ...ees-tee-yo-room
I want a loaf	**Bir ekmek istiyorum** beer ekmek ees-tee-yo-room
I want this	**bunu istiyorum** boo-noo ees-tee-yo-room
I don't want this	**bunu istemiyorum** boo-noo ees-te-mee-yo-room
How much is this?	**Bu ne kadar?** boo ne ka-dar?
How many?	**Kaç tane?** kach ta-ne?
When is...?	**...ne zaman?** ...ne za-man?
When is breakfast?	**Kahvaltı ne zaman?** kah-val-tuh ne za-man?

13

What time is it?	**Saat kaç?** sa-at kach?
At what time...?	**...saat kaçta?** ...sa-at kach-ta?
Where is...?	**...nerede?** ...ne-re-de?
Where is the bank?	**Banka nerede?** ban-ka ne-re-de?
Where is the toilet?	**Tuvalet nerede?** too-va-let ne-re-de?
Which one?	**Hangisi?** han-gee-see?
Why?	**Neden?** ne-den?
Please go away!	**Lütfen gidin!** lewt-fen gee-deen!
Is ... included?	**...dahil mi?** ...da-heel mee?
a/an/one ... please	**bir ... lütfen** beer ... lewt-fen
two beers please	**iki bira lütfen** ee-kee bee-ra lewt-fen
some ... please	**biraz ... lütfen** bee-raz ... lewt-fen

Signs and notices

açık	open
kapalı	closed
bayan	ladies
bay	gentlemen
self-servis	self-service
itiniz	push
çekiniz	pull
kasa	cash desk
içme suyu	drinking water
tuvalet	toilets
boş	vacant
dolu	engaged
acil servis	emergency department
ilk yardım	first aid
dolu	full
dur	stop
bozuk	out of order
kiralık	for hire/rent
satılık	for sale
indirim	sales

bodrum	basement
zemin kat	ground floor
giriş	entrance
gişe	ticket office
karakol	police station
kayıp bürosu	lost property
kalkış	departures
varış	arrivals
yasak	prohibited
emanetçi	left luggage
özel	private
sıcak	hot
soğuk	cold
tehlike	danger
sigara içilmez	no smoking
dokunmayınız	do not touch
çıkış	exit
kabin	changing room
banyo	bathroom
dikkat!	caution!
enformasyon	information
danışma	enquiries

Polite expressions

• •

Good manners are very important to Turkish people. You may see people kissing each other on both cheeks when they meet, but this happens only if they know each other very well. To address someone formally, use **bey** for men or **hanım** for women after their first name e.g. **Mehmet Bey, Fatma Hanım**.

How do you do?	**Nasılsınız?** na-suhl-suh-nuhz?
Pleased to meet you	**Memnun oldum** mem-noon ol-doom
Thank you	**Teşekkür ederim** te-shek-kewr e-de-reem
I am fine	**İyiyim** ee-yee-yeem
Welcome!	**Hoşgeldiniz!** hosh gel-dee-neez!
(reply to 'welcome')	**Hoşbulduk!** hosh bool-dook!
Here you are	**Buyurun** boo-yoo-roon
Pardon?	**Efendim?** e-fen-deem?
This is...	**Bu...** boo...

17

This is my husband/wife	**Bu eşim** boo e-sheem
Enjoy your meal!	**Afiyet Olsun!** a-fee-yet ol-soon!
The meal was delicious	**Yemek çok lezzetliydi** ye-mek chok lez-zet-leey-dee
Thank you very much	**Çok teşekkürler** chok te-shek-kewr-ler
Have a good trip!	**İyi yolculuklar!** ee-yee yol-djoo-look-lar!
Enjoy your holiday!	**İyi tatiller!** ee-yee ta-teel-ler!

Celebrations

. . . .

Happy birthday! (informal)	**Doğum günün kutlu olsun!** do-oom gew-newn koot-loo ol-soon!
Congratulations!	**Tebrikler!** teb-reek-ler!
Cheers! (only when you raise your glass to say cheers!)	**Şerefe!** she-re-fe!
Happy New Year!	**Mutlu yıllar!** moot-loo yuhl-lar!

| Happy Bayram! (for Muslim religious holidays only) | **Mutlu Bayramlar!** moot-loo bay-ram-lar! |

Making friends

• •

FACE TO FACE

Merhaba, Benim adım … Senin adın ne? (informal)/
Sizin adınız ne? (formal)
mer-ha-ba, be-neem a-duhm … se-neen a-duhn ne?/
see-zeen a-duh-nuz ne?
Hello my name is … What's your name?

Nerelisin? (informal)/**Nerelisiniz?** (formal)
ne-re-lee-seen?/ne-re-lee-see-neez?
Where are you from?

İngilizim
Een-gee-lee-zeem
I'm from England

Memnun oldum
mem-noon ol-doom
Nice to meet you

| What's your name? (informal) | **Adın ne?** a-duhn ne? |
| My name is... | **Benim adım…** be-neem a-duhm… |

19

How old are you? (informal)	**Kaç yaşındasın?** kach ya-shuhn-da-suhn?	
I'm ... years old	**...yaşındayım** ...ya-shuhn-da-yuhm	
Where do you live? (informal)	**Nerede oturuyorsun?** ne-re-de o-too-roo-yor-suhn?	
I live...	**...oturuyorum** ...o-too-roo-yo-room	
in London	**Londra'da** lond-ra-da	
in Scotland	**İskoçya'da** ees-koch-ya-da	
Where are you from?	**Nerelisiniz?** ne-re-lee-see-neez?	
I'm English	**İngilizim** een-gee-lee-zeem	
I'm Scottish	**İskoçum** ees-ko-choom	
England/ English	**İngiltere/İngiliz** een-geel-te-re/een-ge-leez	
Scotland/ Scottish	**İskoçya/İskoç** ees-koch-ya/ees-koch	
Wales/Welsh	**Galler/Galli** gall-ler/gall-lee	
Ireland/Irish	**İrlanda/İrlandalı** eer-lan-da/eer-lan-da-luh	

USA/American	**ABD/Amerikalı**
	ah-beh-deh/Ah-meh-ree-kah-luh
Australia/ Australian	**Avustralya/Avustralyalı**
	A-voos-tral-ya/ A-voos-tral-ya-luh
Are you married?	**Evli misiniz?**
	ev-lee mee-see-neez?
Do you have children?	**Çocuklarınız var mı?**
	cho-djook-la-ruh-nuhz var muh?
I have children	**Çocuklarım var**
	cho-djook-la-ruhm var
I have no children	**Çocuğum yok**
	cho-djoo-oom yok
I have a boyfriend	**Erkek arkadaşım var**
	er-kek ar-ka-da-shuhm var
I have a girlfriend	**Kız arkadaşım var**
	kuhz ar-ka-da-shuhm var
I'm single	**Bekârım**
	be-ka-ruhm
I'm married	**Evliyim**
	Ev-lee-yeem
I'm divorced	**Boşandım**
	bo-shan-duhm

Work

What is your job?	**İşiniz ne?**	ee-shee-neez ne?
Do you enjoy it?	**Memnun musunuz?**	mem-noon moo-soo-nooz?
I'm a doctor	**Doktorum**	dok-to-room
I'm a teacher	**Öğretmenim**	ur-ret-me-neem
I'm a nurse	**Hemşireyim**	hem-shee-re-yeem
I work in a shop	**Bir mağazada çalışıyorum**	beer ma-a-za-da cha-luh-shuh-yo-room

Weather

açık a-chuhk		clear
yağmurlu ya-moor-loo		rainy
soğuk so-ook		cold
sıcak suh-djak		hot
güneşli gew-nesh-lee		sunny
nemli nem-lee		humid

It's sunny/raining	**Güneşli/Yağmurlu** gew-nesh-lee/ya-moor-loo
It's windy	**Rüzgarlı** rewz-gar-luh
It's very hot	**Çok sıcak** chok suh-djak
What is the temperature?	**Hava sıcaklığı nedir?** ha-va suh-djak-luh-uh ne-deer?
What is the weather forecast for tomorrow?	**Yarın hava nasıl olacakmış?** ya-ruhn ha-va na-suhl o-la-djak-muhsh?
Does it get cool at night?	**Akşamları serinliyor mu?** ak-sham-la-ruh se-reen-lee-yor moo?
Will there be a storm?	**Fırtına olacak mı?** fuhr-tu-na o-la-djak-muh?
What beautiful weather!	**Ne güzel hava!** ne gew-zel ha-va!
What bad weather!	**Ne kötü hava!** ne kur-tew ha-va!

Getting around

Asking the way

· ·

sol sol	left
sağ sa	right
düz dewz	straight on
karşısında kar-shuh-suhn-dah	opposite
yanında ya-nuhn-dah	next to
trafik ışıkları tra-feek uh-shuhk-la-ruh	traffic lights
köşede kur-she-de	at the corner

FACE TO FACE

Afedersiniz. Postane nerede?
a-fe-der-see-neez. Pos-ta-ne ne-re-de?
Excuse me. Where is the post office?

Düz gidin ve köşede sağa/sola dönün
dewz gee-deen ve kur-she-de sa-a/so-la dur-newn
Keep straight on and turn right/left at the corner

Çok uzak mı?
Chok oo-zak muh?
Is it very far?

Hayır. İki yüz metre/iki dakika ilerde
ha-yuhr. ee-kee yewz met-re/ee-kee da-ki-ka ee-ler-de
No. Only 200 metres/2 minutes away

Teşekkür ederim
te-shek-kewr e-de-reem
Thank you

Birşey değil
beer-shey de-eel
You are welcome

Where is...?	**...nerede?** ...ne-re-de?
Where is the museum?	**Müze nerede?** mew-ze ne-re-de?
How do I get to...?	**...nasıl giderim?** ...na-suhl gee-de-reem?
How do I get to the museum?	**Müzeye nasıl giderim?** mew-ze-ye na-suhl gee-de-reem?
to the coach station	**otogara** o-to-ga-ra
to the beach	**plaja** pla-zha
to my hotel	**otelime** o-te-lee-me
Is it far?	**Uzak mı?** oo-zak muh?

25

Sola dönün so-la dur-newn	Turn left
Sağa dönün sa-a dur-newn	Turn right
Düz devam edin dewz de-vam e-deen	Keep straight on

Bus and coach

Buses and coaches are the cheapest and best way to travel in Turkey. On most routes, you'll need to buy your ticket in advance. Coaches are generally comfortable and refreshments are available at no extra charge. On long routes, coaches normally stop at a site where you can find food, toilets and souvenir shops. Most coach companies run free minibus services from the coach station at your destination to the city centre and other main local areas.

otobüs durağı o-to-bews doo-ra-uh	bus stop
otogar o-to-gar	coach station
bilet bee-let	ticket

| **yolcu otobüsü** yol-djuh o-to-bews-oo | coach |
| **ring seferi** ring se-fuhr-ee | shuttle bus |

FACE TO FACE

Afedersiniz. Hangisi saat yedide İstanbul'a gidecek otobüs?
a-fe-der-see-neez. han-gee-see sa-at ye-dee-de ees-tan-boo-la gee-de-djek o-to-bews?
Excuse me. Which one is the 7 o'clock Istanbul bus?

İleride sağdaki/soldaki.
ee-le-ree-de saa-da-kee/sol-da-kee.
The one on the right/left.

Where is the coach station?	**Otogar nerede?** o-to-gar ne-re-de?
Is there a bus to...?	**...otobüs var mı?** ...o-to-bews var muh?
Does it go to...?	**...gider mi?** ...gee-der mee?
the airport	**havaalanına** ha-va-a-la-nuh-nah
the beach	**plaja** pla-zha
the centre	**şehir merkezine** she-heer mer-ke-zee-ne

27

1 ticket	**bir bilet**
	beer bee-let
2 tickets	**iki bilet**
	ee-kee bee-let
Is there a reduction for children?	**Çocuk indirimi var mı?** cho-djook een-dee-ree-mee var muh?
When is the next bus?	**Bir sonraki otobüs saat kaçta?** beer son-ra-kee o-to-bews sa-at kach-ta?

YOU MAY HEAR...

Otobüs yok o-to-bews yok	There is no bus
Taksi tutmanız gerek tak-see toot-ma-nuhz ge-rek	You must take a taxi

Metro

. . . .

Ankara, Istanbul, Izmir, Bursa and Adana are the only cities with over/underground metro systems at the moment. Istanbul also has an undersea rail tunnel which goes under the Bosphorus, called **Marmaray**, connecting the metro system on either side.

giriş	gee-reesh	entrance
çıkış	chuh-kuhsh	way out

Where is the nearest metro station?	**En yakın metro istasyonu nerede?** en ya-kuhn met-ro ees-tas-yo-noo ne-re-de?
How does the ticket machine work?	**Bilet otomatı nasıl çalışıyor?** bee-let o-to-ma-tuh na-suhl cha-luh-shuh-yor?
Do you have a map of the metro?	**Metro haritası var mı?** me-tro ha-ree-ta-suh var-muh?
How do I/we get to...?	**...nasıl gidebilirim?** ...na-suhl gee-de-bee-lee-reem?
Do I have to change?	**Hat değiştirecek miyim?** hat de-eesh-tee-re-djek mee-yeem?
What is the next stop?	**Bir sonraki durak hangisi?** beer son-ra-kee doo-rak han-gee-see?
Excuse me! I'm getting off here	**Afedersiniz!/Pardon! İneceğim** af-e-der-see-neez!/par-don! ee-ne-dje-eem

Train

You should buy your train ticket in advance, especially on longer routes. A 20% reduction applies to students, teachers, over 60s and disabled people. Return tickets are usually cheaper than two singles. Most long-distance trains have a restaurant coach with a reasonably good menu. There are several public transport cards in major cities. They can be used on buses, ferries, metro, trains and trams. There is the **IETT** card – the Istanbul Transport Card (**İstanbulkart**) and the **IDO** sea transport card (for Istanbul and Izmir).

FACE TO FACE

İzmir'e bir sonraki tren ne zaman?
eez-mee-re beer son-ra-kee tren ne za-man?
When is the next train to Izmir?

Saat yedide (7'de)
sa-at ye-dee-de
At 7 o'clock

Üç bilet lütfen
ewch bee-let lewt-fen
3 tickets please

Tek yön mü, gidiş-dönüş mü?
tek yurn mew, gee-deesh dur-newsh mew?
Single or return?

I've no change	**Bozuğum yok**
	bo-zoo-oom yok
Keep the change	**Üstü kalsın**
	ews-tew kal-suhn

Boat and ferry

A good way of experiencing Istanbul is to take a boat across the Bosphorus. You can purchase tokens (**jeton**) for the boats from machines located at the terminal where you board. You can also use your Istanbul public transport card (**İstanbul**) which can also be bought from kiosks (**gişe**) or vending machines at the terminal. **Şehir Hat**... and **Istanbul Fast Ferries** (**IDO**) provide time... and routes for boats and ferries.

gişe gee-she	ticket office
jeton zhe-ton	token for ferry
tarife ta-ree-fe	timetable
varış va-ruhsh	arrival
kalkış kal-kuhsh	departure
deniz otobüsü de-neez o-to-bew-sew	inter-city sea b...

Gidiş-dönüş lütfen
gee-deesh-dur-newsh lewt-fen
Return please

istasyon ees-tas-yon	station
tren tren	train
peron pe-ron	platform
koltuk kol-took	seat
billet bee-let	ticket
rezervasyon bürosu re-zer-vas-yon bew-ro-soo	booking office
tarife ta-ree-fe	timetable
bağlantı ba-lan-tuh	connection
e-bilet ee-bee-let	e-ticket
e-rezervasyon e-re-zer-vas-yon	e-booking

Where is the station?	**İstasyon nerede?** ees-tas-yon ne-re-de?
a single	**tek yön** tek yurn
2 singles	**iki tane tek yön** ee-kee ta-ne tek yurn
a return	**bir tane gidiş-dönüş** beer ta-ne gee-deesh-dur-newsh

2 returns	**iki tane gidiş-dönüş**
	ee-kee ta-ne gee-deesh-dur-newsh
a child's ticket	**çocuk bileti**
	cho-djook bee-le-tee
first class	**birinci mevki**
	bee-reen-djee mev-kee
second class	**ikinci mevki**
	ee-keen-djee mev-kee
I booked online	**İnternetle rezervasyon yaptım**
	een-ter-net-le re-zer-vas-yon yap-tuhm
I want to book a seat	**Bir yer ayırtmak istiyorum**
	beer yer a-yuhrt-mak ees-tee-yo-room
Which platform?	**Hangi peron?**
	han-gee pe-ron?
When does it leave?	**Ne zaman kalkıyor?**
	ne za-man kal-kuh-yor?
When does it arrive?	**Ne zaman varıyor?**
	ne za-man va-ruh-yor?
Is this seat free?	**Bu koltuk boş mu?**
	boo kol-took bosh moo?

Taxi

Official taxis in Turkey are yellow. There are also mini cab services in major cities. Most taxis (**taksi**) have meters, but it's wise to check the price before a long journey. In larger cities, you should give the exact address of the destination, and try to note landmarks too. Alternatively, there are **dolmus**, minibuses for journeys over short distances. The fare and destination will be displayed on the front window. You can get off anywhere on the route by shouting **Musait bir yerde!** (mew-sa-eet beer yer-de!) or **İnebilirmiyim?** (ee-nuhr-bee-leer-mee-yeem?)

Where can I get a taxi?	**Nerede taksi bulabilirim?**
	ne-re-de tak-see boo-la-bee-lee-reem?
I want to go to...	**...gitmek istiyorum**
	...geet-mek ees-tee-yo-room
How much is it?	**Ne kadar?**
	ne ka-dar?
To the airport, please	**Havaalanı, lütfen**
	ha-va-a-la-nuh, lewt-fen
To the beach, please	**Plaja, lütfen**
	pla-zha, lewt-fen
Please stop here	**Burada durun, lütfen**
	boo-ra-da doo-roon, lewt-fen

Gidiş-dönüş lütfen
gee-deesh-dur-newsh lewt-fen
Return please

istasyon ees-tas-yon	station
tren tren	train
peron pe-ron	platform
koltuk kol-took	seat
billet bee-let	ticket
rezervasyon bürosu re-zer-vas-yon bew-ro-soo	booking office
tarife ta-ree-fe	timetable
bağlantı ba-lan-tuh	connection
e-bilet ee-bee-let	e-ticket
e-rezervasyon e-re-zer-vas-yon	e-booking

Where is the station?	**İstasyon nerede?** ees-tas-yon ne-re-de?
a single	**tek yön** tek yurn
2 singles	**iki tane tek yön** ee-kee ta-ne tek yurn
a return	**bir tane gidiş-dönüş** beer ta-ne gee-deesh-dur-newsh

2 returns	**iki tane gidiş-dönüş**	ee-kee ta-ne gee-deesh-dur-newsh
a child's ticket	**çocuk bileti**	cho-djook bee-le-tee
first class	**birinci mevki**	bee-reen-djee mev-kee
second class	**ikinci mevki**	ee-keen-djee mev-kee
I booked online	**İnternetle rezervasyon yaptım**	een-ter-net-le re-zer-vas-yon yap-tuhm
I want to book a seat	**Bir yer ayırtmak istiyorum**	beer yer a-yuhrt-mak ees-tee-yo-room
Which platform?	**Hangi peron?**	han-gee pe-ron?
When does it leave?	**Ne zaman kalkıyor?**	ne za-man kal-kuh-yor?
When does it arrive?	**Ne zaman varıyor?**	ne za-man va-ruh-yor?
Is this seat free?	**Bu koltuk boş mu?**	boo kol-took bosh moo?

Taxi

. . . .

Official taxis in Turkey are yellow. There are also
mini cab services in major cities. Most taxis (**taksi**)
have meters, but it's wise to check the price before
a long journey. In larger cities, you should give the
exact address of the destination, and try to note
landmarks too. Alternatively, there are **dolmus**,
minibuses for journeys over short distances. The
fare and destination will be displayed on the front
window. You can get off anywhere on the route by
shouting **Musait bir yerde!** (mew-sa-eet beer yer-de!)
or **İnebilirmiyim?** (ee-nuhr-bee-leer-mee-yeem?)

Where can I get a taxi?	**Nerede taksi bulabilirim?** ne-re-de tak-see boo-la-bee-lee-reem?
I want to go to...	**...gitmek istiyorum** ...geet-mek ees-tee-yo-room
How much is it?	**Ne kadar?** ne ka-dar?
To the airport, please	**Havaalanı, lütfen** ha-va-a-la-nuh, lewt-fen
To the beach, please	**Plaja, lütfen** pla-zha, lewt-fen
Please stop here	**Burada durun, lütfen** boo-ra-da doo-roon, lewt-fen

I've no change	**Bozuğum yok**
	bo-zoo-oom yok
Keep the change	**Üstü kalsın**
	ews-tew kal-suhn

Boat and ferry

. . . .

A good way of experiencing Istanbul is to take a
boat across the Bosphorus. You can purchase
tokens (**jeton**) for the boats from machines located
at the terminal where you board. You can also use
your Istanbul public transport card (**İstanbulkart**),
which can also be bought from kiosks (**gişe**) or
vending machines at the terminal. **Şehir Hatları**
and **Istanbul Fast Ferries** (**İDO**) provide timetables
and routes for boats and ferries.

gişe	gee-she	ticket office
jeton	zhe-ton	token for ferry
tarife	ta-ree-fe	timetable
varış	va-ruhsh	arrival
kalkış	kal-kuhsh	departure
deniz otobüsü de-neez o-to-bew-sew		inter-city sea bus

1 token	**bir jeton**	
	beer zhe-ton	
2 tokens	**iki jeton**	
	ee-kee zhe-ton	
When is the next boat?	**Bir sonraki vapur saat kaçta?**	
	beer son-ra-kee va-poor sa-at kach-tah?	
When is the last boat?	**En son vapur saat kaçta?**	
	en son va-poor sa-at kach-tah?	
Is there a sea bus?	**Deniz otobüsü var mı?**	
	de-neez o-to-bew-sew var muh?	
Is there a timetable?	**Tarife var mı?**	
	ta-ree-fe var muh?	
How long does it take?	**Ne kadar sürer?**	
	ne ka-dar sew-rer?	

Air travel

. . . .

The major airports in Turkey are **İstanbul Atatürk** Airport, **İstanbul Sabiha Gökçen** Airport, **Antalya** Airport, **İzmir Adnan Menderes** Airport and **Dalaman** Airport in Muğla.

havaalanı	airport
ha-va-a-la-nuh	
kapı ka-puh	gate

35

iniş (geliş) ee-neesh	arrivals
kalkış (gidiş) kal-kuhsh	departures
uçuş oo-choosh	flight
iç hat eech hat	domestic
dış hat duhsh hat	international
danışma da-nuhsh-ma	information

Where can I print my ticket? **Biletimin çıktısını nereden alabilirim?**
bee-let-ee-meen chuk-tuh-suh-nuh ne-re-den a-la-bee-lee-reem?

I have my boarding pass on my smartphone **Biniş kartım akıllı telefonumda** bee-neesh kar-tuhm a-kul-luh te-le-fo-nuhm-da

My flight is at ... o'clock **Uçağım saat ... 'da** oo-cha-uhm sa-at ... da

When will the flight leave? **Uçak ne zaman kalkıyor?** oo-chak ne za-man kal-kuh-yor?

checked luggage **kontrol edilmiş bagaj** kon-trol e-deel-meesh ba-gazh

hand luggage **el bagajı** el ba-ga-zhuh

YOU MAY HEAR...

...nolu kapıya gidiniz ...no-loo ka-puh-ya gee-dee-neez	Go to gate number...
Sıvı maddeyle girilmez suh-vuh mad-day-le gee-reel-mez	No liquids
Bagajınız azami ağırlığı aşıyor ba-ga-zhuh-nuz a-za-mee a-uhr-luhr-uh a-shuh-yor	Your luggage exceeds the maximum weight
Son çağrı son chah-ruh	Last call
Ertelendi er-te-len-dee	Delayed

Customs control

pasaport pa-sa-port	passport
gümrük gewm-rewk	customs
alkol al-kol	alcohol
sigara see-ga-ra	tobacco

Do I have to pay duty on this?	**Bunun için gümrük ödemem gerekiyor mu?** boo-noon ee-cheen gewm-rewk ur-de-mem ge-re-kee-yor-moo?

It is my medicine	**Bu benim ilacım**
	boo be-neem ee-la-djuhm
I bought this duty-free	**Bunu gümrüksüz aldım**
	boo-noo gewm-rewk-sewz al-duhm

Car hire

. . . .

There are rental agencies in all main towns.
A cash deposit will be required if you are not paying
by credit card. When hiring with a British driving
licence, it is valid in Turkey without any age limit or
restriction on how long the licence has to have
been held.

anahtarlar	a-nah-tar-lar	keys
sigorta belgeleri see-gor-ta bel-ge-le-ree		insurance documents
ehliyet	eh-lee-yet	driving licence

I want to hire a car	**Araba kiralamak istiyorum**
	a-ra-ba kee-ra-la-mak
	ees-tee-yo-room
with automatic gears	**otomatik vitesli**
	o-to-ma-teek vee-tes-lee
for 1 day	**bir günlüğüne**
	beer gewn-lew-ew-ne

for 2 days	**iki günlüğüne**
	ee-kee gewn-lew-ew-ne
How much is it?	**Ne kadar?**
	ne ka-dar?
Is insurance included?	**Sigorta dahil mi?**
	see-gor-ta da-heel mee?
Is there a deposit to pay?	**Depozit vermek gerekiyor mu?**
	de-po-zeet ver-mek ge-re-kee-yor moo?
Can I pay by credit card?	**Kredi kartı ile ödeyebilir miyim?**
	kre-dee kar-tuh ee-le ur-de-ye-bee-leer mee-yeem?
What petrol does it take?	**Ne tür benzin alır?**
	ne tewr ben-zeen a-luhr?

Driving and petrol

• •

You must carry the following equipment: two warning triangles, first aid kit, tool kit, tow rope and fire extinguisher. Driving at night is not recommended because of the lack of road markings, and the danger of hitting unlit tractors, pedestrians and animals.

| Can I park here? | **Buraya park edebilir miyim?** |
| | boo-ra-ya park e-de-bee-leer mee-yeem? |

| We are driving to... | ...gidiyoruz
...gee-dee-yo-rooz |
| How long will it take? | **Ne kadar sürer?**
ne ka-dar sew-rer? |

Çok hızlı sürüyorsunuz chok huhz-luh sew-rew-yor-soo-nooz	You are driving too fast
Ehliyetiniz lütfen eh-lee-ye-tee-neez lewt-fen	Your driving licence please
...yok ...yok	We have no...
Yağ/Su/Hava lazım ya/soo/ha-va la-zuhm	You need oil/water/air

Where is the nearest petrol station?	**En yakın benzin istasyonu nerede?** en ya-kuhn ben-zeen ees-tas-yo-noo ne-re-de?
Fill it up, please	**Depoyu doldurun, lütfen** de-po-yoo dol-doo-roon lewt-fen
unleaded	**kurşunsuz** koor-shoon-sooz
diesel	**dizel** dee-zel
Please check the oil	**Yağını kontrol eder misiniz?** ya-uh-nuh kon-trol e-der mee-see-neez?

dikkat deek-kat	caution/danger
dur door	stop
otoyol o-to-yol	motorway
şehir merkezi she-heer mer-ke-zee	town centre

Breakdown

. . . .

If you have a breakdown on the motorway,
go to the nearest service station and ask for help.
By law you are required to carry two red breakdown
triangles. The Turkish Tourism and Automobile Club
(**TTOK**) provides roadside assistance and breakdown
services as well as travel advice. Check your home
breakdown insurance policy to see if it covers the
whole of Turkey, or only covers some regions.

My car has broken down	**Arabam bozuldu** a-ra-bam bo-zool-doo
Can you help me?	**Yardım edebilir misiniz?** yar-duhm e-de-bee-leer mee-see-neez?
I've run out of petrol	**Benzinim bitti** ben-zee-neem beet-tee
I have a flat tyre	**Lastiğim patladı** las-tee-eem pat-la-duh

41

Where is the nearest garage (repair shop)?	**En yakın tamirhane nerede?** en ya-kuhn ta-meer-ha-ne ne-re-de?
Can you repair it?	**Tamir edebilir misiniz?** ta-meer e-de-bee-leer mee-see-neez?
How long will it take?	**Ne kadar sürer?** ne ka-dar sew-rer?
How much will it cost?	**Ne kadar tutar?** ne ka-dar too-tar?

Car parts

. . . .

Local garages will have no trouble repairing your car very quickly. Repairs are carried out in industrial zones, called **sanayi**, located on the outskirts of towns.

| The ... doesn't work | **...çalışmıyor** ...cha-luhsh-muh-yor |
| Where is the repair shop? | **tamirhane nerede?** ta-meer-ha-ne ne-re-de? |

accelerator	**gaz pedalı**	gaz pe-da-luh
alternator	**alternatör**	al-ter-na-tur
battery	**akü**	a-kew
brakes	**frenler**	f-ren-ler
choke	**jikle**	zheek-le

clutch	**debriyaj**	deb-ree-yazh
engine	**motor**	mo-tor
exhaust pipe	**eksoz borusu**	ek-soz bo-roo-soo
fuse	**sigorta**	see-gor-ta
gears	**vitesler**	vee-tes-ler
handbrake	**el freni**	el fre-nee
headlights	**farlar**	far-lar
ignition	**kontak**	kon-tak
ignition key	**kontak anahtarı**	kon-tak a-nah-ta-ruh
indicator	**gösterge**	gurs-ter-ge
lock	**kilit**	kee-leet
radiator	**radyatör**	rad-ya-tur
reverse gear	**geri vites**	ge-ree vee-tes
seat belt	**emniyet kemeri**	em-nee-yet ke-me-ree
spark plug	**buji**	boo-zhee
steering wheel	**direksiyon**	dee-rek-see-yon
tyre	**lastik**	las-teek
wheel	**tekerlek**	te-ker-lek
windscreen	**ön cam**	urn djam
windscreen wiper	**cam sileceği**	djam see-le-djee-ee

Road signs

TEK YÖN

ahead only

stop

SOLA DÖN

turn left

SAĞA DÖN

turn right

GİRİLMEZ

no entry

use of horn
prohibited

OTOYOL
motorway

HIZINI AZALT
reduce speed

YAYA GEÇİDİ
pedestrian crossing

GİRİŞ
entrance

ÇIKIŞ
exit

ŞEHİR MERKEZİ
city centre

YOL
road

BENZİN
petrol

north

kuzey

batı — west

doğu — east

güney

south

Staying somewhere

Hotel (booking)

Hotels are rated from 1 to 5 stars, although unstarred hotels also exist. In tourist areas it's easy to find a **pansiyon** or guesthouse. Breakfast will probably not be included in the room price. However, in tourist hotels and holiday resorts, breakfast is usually included – half board, full board and all-inclusive options are available.

FACE TO FACE

Tek/çift kişilik bir oda istiyoruz
Tek/cheeft kee-shee-leek beer o-da ees-tee-yo-ruz
We would like to book a single/double room

Kaç gecelik?
Kach ge-dje-leek?
For how many nights?

Bir gece/iki gece/bir hafta için
Beer ge-dje/ee-kee ge-dje/beer haf-ta ee-cheen
For one night/two nights/one week

Do you have a room?	**Boş odanız var mı?** bosh o-da-nuhz var muh?

I'd like...	**...istiyorum** ...ees-tee-yo-room
a single room	**tek kişilik oda** tek kee-shee-leek o-da
a double room	**çift kişilik oda** cheeft kee-shee-leek o-da
a cot	**bebek yatağl** be-bek ya-ta-uh
with shower	**duşlu** doosh-loo
with bath	**banyolu** ban-yo-loo
How much is it per night?	**Gecelik ücreti ne kadar?** ge-dje-leek ewdj-re-tee ne ka-dar?
1 night	**bir gece** beer ge-dje
2 nights	**iki gece** ee-kee ge-dje
I want a room on the ground floor	**Zemin katta bir oda istiyorum** ze-meen kat-ta beer o-da ees-tee-yo-room

YOU MAY HEAR...

İsminiz, lütfen/Adınız lütfen ees-mee-neez, lewt-fen/ a-duh-nuhz lewt-fen	Your name, please

47

Pasaportunuz, lütfen pa-sa-por-too-nooz, lewt-fen	Your passport, please
Doluyuz do-loo-yooz	We are full
telefonla rezervasyon te-le-fon-la re-zer-vas-yon	by phone

Hotel desk

. . . .

I have a reservation	**Rezervasyonum var** re-zer-vas-yo-noom var
My name is...	**İsmim...** ees-meem...
Have you a different room?	**Başka odanız var mı?** bash-ka o-da-nuhz var muh?
Where can I park the car?	**Arabamı nereye park edebilirim?** a-ra-ba-muh ne-re-ye park e-de-bee-lee-reem?
What time is breakfast?	**Kahvaltı saat kaçta?** kah-val-tuh sa-at kach-ta?
What time is dinner?	**Akşam yemeği saat kaçta?** ak-sham ye-me-ee sa-at kach-ta?
The key, please	**Anahtar, lütfen** a-na-tar, lewt-fen

Room number...	**Oda numarası...**
	o-da noo-ma-ra-suh...
I'm leaving tomorrow	**Yarın ayrılıyorum**
	ya-ruhn ay-ruh-luh-yo-room
I reserved the room(s) online	**Odayı (odaları) internette ayırttım**
	o-da-yuh (o-da-lar-uh) een-ter-net-te a-yurt-tuhm
Does the price include breakfast?	**Fiyata kahvaltı dahil mi?**
	fee-ya-ta kah-val-tuh da-heel mee?
Is there a hotel restaurant/bar	**Otel'de bir restoran/bar var mı?**
	o-tel-de beer res-to-ran/bar var-muh?
Is there a toilet for disabled people?	**Engelliler için tuvalet var mı?**
	en-gel-lee-ler ee-cheen too-va-let var muh?
Where is the lift?	**Asansör nerede?**
	a-san-sur ne-re-de?

Camping

• •

A list of registered campsites can be obtained from tourist offices in Turkey. European campsite specialist **ASCI** also has a list of campsites in Turkey, which are inspected annually.

kamp yeri/kamping kamp ye-ree/kam-ping	camp site
içme suyu eech-me soo-yoo	drinking water
duşlar doosh-lar	showers
müdüriyet mew-dew-ree-yet	office
resepsiyon re-sep-see-yon	reception
çadır cha-duhr	tent

Where is the campsite?	**Kamp yeri nerede?** kamp ye-ree ne-re-de?	
How much is it per night?	**Geceliği ne kadar?** ge-dje-lee-ee ne ka-dar?	
1 night	**bir gece** beer ge-dje	
2 nights	**iki gece** ee-kee ge-dje	
toilets	**tuvalet** too-va-let	
shower	**duş** doosh	
drinking water	**içme suyu** eech-me soo-yoo	
Where's the...?	**...nerede?** ...ne-re-de?	

50

Doluyuz do-loo-yooz | We are full

Self-catering

· ·

Can you give us an extra set of keys, please?	**Yedek anahtar verir misiniz, lütfen?** ye-dek a-nah-tar ve-reer mee-see-neez, lewt-fen?
Who do we contact if there are problems?	**Bir problem çıkarsa kiminle görüşelim?** beer prob-lem chuh-kar-sa kee-meen-le gur-rew-she-leem?
How does the heating work?	**Kombi/Şofben nasıl çalışıyor?** kom-bee/shof-ben na-suhl cha-luh-shuh-yor?
Is there always hot water?	**Her saat sıcak su var mı?** her sa-at suh-djak soo var muh?
Where is the nearest supermarket?	**En yakın market nerede?** en ya-kuhn mar-ket ne-re-de?
Where do we leave the rubbish?	**Çöpü nereye bırakalım?** chur-pew ne-re-ye buh-ra-ka-luhm?
recycling	**geri dönüşüm** ge-ree duh-nuh-shum

51

Shopping

Shopping phrases

Shops are generally open from 9 a.m. to 7 p.m. Monday to Saturday and closed on Sunday. Some shops close for lunch between 12 and 2 p.m. In tourist towns, the shops are open for longer, with no lunch break.

Good-natured haggling is the norm: offer half to two-thirds of the asking price, then settle on a price somewhere in between. Don't offer unless you are serious; to settle on a price and then not buy is considered bad manners. Once a week most towns have a farmers' market (**Pazar**) mainly for locally grown fresh fruit and vegetables. You can haggle when shopping but do not haggle at farmers' markets for produce prices.

Where are the shops, please?	**Çarşı nerede, lütfen?** char-shuh ne-re-de, lewt-fen?
I'm looking for...	**...arıyorum** ...a-ruh-yo-room

FACE TO FACE

Kaç beden giyiyorsunuz?
kach be-den gee-yee-yor-soo-nooz?
What is your size?

Otuz sekiz/kırk beden
o-tooz se-keez/kuhrk be-den
Size 38/40

Where is the nearest...?	**En yakın ... nerede?** en ya-kuhn ... ne-re-de?
Where is the market?	**Pazar nerede?** Pa-zar ne-re-de?
When does it close?	**Ne zaman kapanır?** ne za-man ka-pa-nur?
How much is it?	**Ne kadar?** ne ka-dar?
It's too expensive	**Çok pahalı** chok pa-ha-luh
I don't want it	**İstemiyorum** ees-te-mee-yo-room

Shops

. . . .

Where is...?	...nerede?
	...ne-re-de?

Where is the baker's?	Fırın nerede?
	fuh-ruhn ne-re-de?

baker's	fırın	fuh-ruhn
bookshop	kitabevi	kee-ta-be-vee
butcher's	kasap	ka-sap
cake shop	pastane	pas-ta-ne
clothes shop	butik	boo-teek
grocer's	bakkal	bak-kal
hairdresser's	kuaför	koo-a-fur
jeweller's	kuyumcu	koo-yoom-djoo
market	pazar	pa-zar
newsagent's	gazete bayii	ga-ze-te ba-yee-ee
optician's	gözlükçü	gurz-lewk-chew
pharmacy	eczane	edj-za-ne
shoe shop	ayakkabıcı	a-yak-ka-buh-djuh
shop	dükkan	dewk-kan
shopping centre	alışveriş merkezi	a-luhsh-ve-reesh mer-ke-zee

spice/herb shop	baharatcı	ba-haa-rat-djuh
souvenir shop	hediyelik eşya dükkanı	he-dee-ye-leek esh-ya doo-ka-nuh
stationer's	kırtasiye	kuhr-ta-see-ye
supermarket	süpermarket	sew-per mar-ket
tobacconist's	tekel bayii	te-kel ba-yee-ee
toy shop	oyuncakçı	o-yoon-djak-chuh

Food (general)

· ·

You can buy most of these from shops labelled
market/süpermarket.

biscuits	bisküvi	bees-kew-vee
bread	ekmek	ek-mek
butter	tereyağı	te-re-ya-uh
cakes	kek	kek
cheese	peynir	pey-neer
chicken	tavuk	ta-vook
chocolate	çikolata	chee-ko-la-ta
coffee (instant)	Nescafé®	nes-ka-fe
coffee	kahve	kah-ve

crisps	cips	cheeps
egg	yumurta	yoo-moor-ta
fish	balık	ba-luhk
flour	un	oon
honey	bal	bal
jam	reçel	re-chel
margarine	margarin	mar-ga-reen
marmalade	marmelat	mar-me-lat
milk	süt	sewt
olive oil	zeytin yağı	zey-teen ya-uh
orange juice	portakal suyu	por-ta-kal soo-yoo
pasta	makarna	ma-kar-na
pepper (seasoning)	karabiber	ka-ra-bee-ber
rice	pirinç	pee-reench
salt	tuz	tooz
stock cubes	et bulyon	et bool-yon
sugar	şeker	she-ker
tea	çay	chay
vinegar	sirke	seer-ke
yoghurt	yoğurt	yo-oort

Food (fruit and veg)

apples	**elma**	el-ma
apricots	**kayısı**	ka-yuh-suh
aubergine	**patlıcan**	pat-luh-djan
bananas	**muz**	mooz
cabbage	**lahana**	la-ha-na
carrots	**havuç**	ha-vooch
cauliflower	**karnıbahar**	kar-nuh-ba-har
cherries	**kiraz**	kee-raz
courgettes	**kabak**	ka-bak
cucumber	**salatalık**	sa-la-ta-luhk
dates	**hurma**	hoor-ma
figs	**incir**	een-djeer
garlic	**sarımsak**	sa-ruhm-sak
grapefruit	**greyfurt**	grey-foort
grapes	**üzüm**	ew-zewm
green beans	**yeşil fasulye**	ye-sheel fa-sool-ye
lemon	**limon**	lee-mon
lettuce	**marul**	ma-rool
melon	**kavun**	ka-voon
mushrooms	**mantar**	man-tar
nectarines	**nektarin**	nek-tar-een
onions	**soğan**	so-an

oranges	portakal	por-ta-kal
peaches	şeftali	shef-ta-lee
pears	armut	ar-moot
peas	bezelye	be-zel-ye
peppers	biber	bee-ber
pineapple	ananas	a-na-nas
plums	erik	e-reek
pomegranate	nar	nar
potatoes	patates	pa-ta-tes
sour cherries	vişne	veesh-ne
spinach	ıspanak	uhs-pa-nak
strawberries	çilek	chee-lek
tomatoes	domates	do-ma-tes
watermelon	karpuz	kar-pooz

Clothes

women's sizes		men's suit sizes		shoe sizes			
UK	EU	UK	EU	UK	EU	UK	EU
8	36	36	46	2	35	7	40
10	38	38	48	3	36	8	41
12	40	40	50	4	37	9	42
14	42	42	52	5	38	10	43
16	44	44	54	6	39	11	44
18	46	46	56				

FACE TO FACE

Bunu deneyebilir miyim?
boo-noo de-ne-ye-bee-leer mee-yeem?
Can I try this one on?

Evet, tabii, burada deneyebilirsiniz
e-vet, ta-bee, boo-ra-da de-ne-ye-bee-leer-see-neez
Yes, of course, you can try it on in here

Bunun ufak/orta/küçük boyu var mı?
boo-noon oo-fak/or-ta/kew-chewk bo-yoo var muh?
Do you have this one in small/medium/large?

Evet var/Hayır yok
e-vet var/ha-yuhr yok
Yes, there is/No, there isn't

It's too big	**Çok büyük**	
	chok bew-yewk	
It's too small	**Çok küçük**	
	chok kew-chewk	

Clothes (articles)

coat	**palto**	pal-to
cotton	**yünlü**	yoon-loo
dress	**elbise**	el-bee-se
hat	**şapka**	shap-ka
jacket	**ceket**	dje-ket
knickers	**kadın külotu**	ka-dın kew-lo-too
leather	**deri**	de-ree
sandals	**sandalet**	san-da-let
shirt	**gömlek**	gurm-lek
shorts	**şort**	short
silk	**ipek**	ee-pek
skirt	**etek**	e-tek
socks	**çorap**	cho-rap
swimsuit	**mayo**	ma-yo
T-shirt	**tişört**	tee-shurt
trousers	**pantolon**	pan-to-lon
underpants	**erkek külotu**	er-kek kew-lo-too
wool	**yün**	yewn

Maps and guides

. . . .

The local tourist information office will usually be
able to provide local maps. The word for map is
harita (ha-ree-ta).

Where can I buy a map?	**Nereden harita alabilirim?** ne-re-den ha-ree-ta a-la-bee-lee-reem?
Do you have a road map?	**Yol haritanız var mı?** yol ha-ree-ta-nuhz var muh?
Do you have a town plan?	**Şehir planı var mı?** she-heer pla-nuh var muh?
Do you have a leaflet/guidebook in English?	**İngilizce broşür/rehber var mı?** een-gee-leez-dje bro-shewr/ reh-ber var muh?
Can you show me where ... is on the map?	**Haritada ... gösterebilir misiniz?** ha-ree-ta-da ... gurs-te-re-bee-leer mee-see-neez?

Post office

. . . .

Post offices are usually open Monday to Friday
8.30 a.m. to 5.30 p.m. with an hour off for lunch
between 12.30 and 1.30 p.m., but keep much longer
hours in large cities.

uçak postası oo-chak pos-ta-suh	airmail
yurt dışı yoort duh-shuh	overseas
yurt içi yoort ee-chee	inland
şehiriçi she-heer ee-chee	local
mektup mek-toop	letter
kart/kartpostal kart/kart-pos-tal	postcard
pul pool	stamps

Where is the post office?	Postane nerede? pos-ta-ne ne-re-de?
5 stamps	beş pul besh pool
for postcards	kartpostal için kart-pos-tal ee-cheen
to Britain	İngiltere'ye een-geel-te-re-ye
to America	Amerika'ya a-me-ree-ka-ya
to Australia	Avusturalya'ya a-voos-tral-ya-ya

62

Technology

hafıza kartı ha-fuh-za kar-tuh	memory card
çıktı almak chuk-tuh al-mak	to print
dijital fotoğraf makinesi dee-zhee-tal fo-to-raf ma-kee-ne-seeh	digital camera
e-sigara e-see-ga-ra	e-cigarette

I need a memory card for this camera	**Bu makine için hafıza kartı** **istiyorum** boo ma-kee-ne ee-chen ha-fuh-za kar-tuh ees-tee-yo-room
I need batteries for this	**Bunun için pil istiyorum** boo-noon ee-cheen peel ees-tee-yo-room
Can you repair...?	**...tamir edebilir misiniz?** ...ta-meer e-de-beeleer-mee- suh-nuz?
my screen	**ekranimi** ek-ra-nuh-muh
my keypad	**klavyemi** klav-ye-mee
my lens	**objektifimi** ob-djek-tee-fee-mee
my charger	**şarj aletimi** sharzh a-let-ee-mee

I want to print my photos	**Fotoğraflarımı bastırmak istiyorum**
	fo-to-raf-la-ruh-mu bas-tuhr-mak ees-tee-yo-room
I have it on my USB	**USB hafıza ünitemde var**
	you-es-bee ha-fuh-za oo-nee-tem-de var
I have it on my e-mail	**e-postamda var**
	e-pos-tam-da var

Leisure

Sightseeing and tourist office

enformasyon/danışma en-for-mas-yon/ da-nuhsh-mah	information
turizm bürosu too-reezm bew-ro-soo	tourist office
rehberli tur reh-ber-lee toor	guided tour
bilet bee-let	tickets
tuvalet too-va-let	toilet

Where is the tourist office?	**Turizm bürosu nerede?** too-ree-zeem bew-ro-soo ne-re-de?
What can we visit in the area?	**Bu bölgede nereyi gezebiliriz?** boo burl-ge-de ne-re-yee ge-ze-bee-lee-reez?
Have you got details in English?	**İngilizce bilgi var mı?** een-gee-leez-dje beel-gee var muh?

65

Are there any excursions?	**Geziler var mı?**
	ge-zee-ler var muh?
Is it OK to take children?	**Çocukları da götürebilir miyiz?**
	cho-djook-lar-uh da
	gur-tew-re-bee-leer mee-yeez?

Entertainment

Big hotels and holiday villages often have dinner shows, which may feature belly dancing. In major cities you will find opera houses, concert halls, theatres and cinemas. Turkey's large cities are hubs for various cultural festivals. Istanbul is host to a biennale, as well as annual film, theatre and jazz festivals. You can find out more information from the Istanbul Foundation for Culture and Arts (**IKSV**).

What is there to do in the evenings?	**Burada akşamları eğlenmek için ne var?**
	boo-ra-da ak-sham-la-ruh
	ey-len-mek ee-cheen ne var?
Is there anywhere we can go to hear live music?	**Canlı müzik olan bir yer var mı?**
	djan-luh mew-zeek o-lan beer yer
	var muh?

| Is there anywhere we can go to see belly dancing? | **Dansöz olan bir yer var mı?** dan-surz o-lan beer yer var muh? |

Nightlife

· ·

Where can I go clubbing?	**Nerede gece kulübü bulabilirim?** ne-re-de ge-je kuh-lew-bew buh-la-bee-lee-reem?	
gay bar/club	**gay bar/ gay kulübü**	gay bar/ gay kuh-lew-bew
gig/concert	**gösteri**	gers-te-ree
music festival	**müzik festivali**	moo-zeek fes-tee-va-lee
nightclub	**gece kulübü**	ge-je kuh-lew-bew
party	**parti**	par-tee
pub, bar	**bar**	bar

Out and about

. . . .

plaj plazh	beach
tehlike teh-lee-ke	danger
duş doosh	showers

Are there any good beaches round here?
Buralarda iyi bir plaj var mı?
boo-ra-lar-da ee-yee beer plazh var muh?

Can I visit in a wheelchair?
Tekerlekli sandalye ile ziyaret edebilir miyim?
te-ker-lek-lee san-dal-ye ee-le zee-ya-ret e-de-bee-leer mee-yeem?

What's on at the cinema?
Sinemada ne oynuyor?
see-ne-ma-da ne oy-noo-yor?

Do you have a guide to local walks?
Bölgedeki yürüyüş yerleri hakkında rehber var mı?
burl-ge-de-kee yew-rew-yewsh yer-le-ree hak-kuhn-da reh-ber var muh?

How many kilometres is the walk?
Yürüyüş toplam kaç kilometre?
yew-rew-yewsh top-lam kach kee-lo-met-re?

adventure centre
serüven parkı
se-ruh-ven park-uh

art gallery
sanat galerisi
sa-nat ga-le-ree-see

Leisure

boat hire	**tekne kiralamak**	tek-ne kee-ra-la-mak
camping	**kampçılık**	kamp-chuh-luk
museum	**müze**	moo-ze
piercing	**delme**	del-me
tattoo	**dövme**	duhv-me
theme park	**tema parkı**	te-ma par-kuh
water park	**su parkı**	soo par-kuh
zoo	**hayvanat bahçesi**	hay-va-nat bah-cheh-see

YOU MAY HEAR...	
Yüzmek yasaktır yooz-mek ya-sak-tuhr	No swimming
Suya atlamak yasaktır soo-ya at-la-mak ya-sak-tuhr	No diving

Music

. . . .

| Are there any concerts? | **Hiç konser var mı?** heech kon-ser var muh? |
| Where can we hear some classical music/ jazz? | **Nerede klasik müzik/jazz dinleyebiliriz?** nee-re-de kla-seek mew-zeek/ caz deen-le-ye-bee-lee-reez? |

folk	**halk müzüği**	halk-moo-zee-ee
hip-hop	**hip-hop**	hip-hop
pop	**pop**	pop
reggae	**rege**	re-ge
rock	**rock**	rok
techno	**tekno**	tek-no

Mosque

. . . .

Women should have their head covered and both
men and women should avoid wearing shorts.
You will have to leave your shoes at the entrance.
Prayers take place five times a day and it would be
best to wait until these are over before entering.

cami dja-mee	mosque
müslüman mews-lew-man	muslim
ayakkabı a-yak-ka-buh	shoes
fotoğraf çekmek yasak fo-to-raf chek-mek ya-sak	no photos
kamera yasak ka-me-ra ya-sak	no videos

When can we see the mosque?	**Camiyi ne zaman görebiliriz?** dja-mee-yee ne za-man guh-re-bee-lee-reez?

Where is the mosque?	**Cami nerede?** dja-mee ne-re-de?

Sport

. . . .

Where can we play tennis/ golf/football?	**Nerede tenis/golf/futbol oynayabiliriz?** ne-re-de te-nees/golf/foot-bol oy-na-ya-bee-lee-reez?
Can we hire racquets/golf clubs?	**Raket/golf sopası kiralayabilir miyiz?** ra-ket/golf so-pa-suh kee-ra-la-ya-bee-leer mee-yeez?
I want to try...	**...denemek istiyorum** ...de-ne-mek ees-tee-yo-rum
I've never done this before	**Bunu daha önce hiç yapmadım** boo-noo da-ha uhn-je heech yap-ma-duhm
How much is it per hour?	**Saati ne kadar?** sa-a-tee ne- ka-dar?
cycling	**bisikletçilik** bee-seek-let-chee-leek
dancing	**dans (etmek)** dans (et-mek)
kayaking	**kayaking** ka-ya-king
rock climbing	**kayalıklara tırmanma** ka-yak-luhk-la-ra tuhr-man-ma

snowboarding	**kar sörfü**	kar suhr-foo
volleyball	**voleybol**	vo-ley-bol
water-skiing	**su kayağı**	soo ka-ya-uh
windsurfing	**rüzgar sörfü**	rooz-gar suhr-foo

Turkish baths

There are separate times, days and often separate baths for men and women. In tourist towns, some baths are mixed. You will be given a couple of towels, wooden bath clogs, and then shown to the changing room to undress. Wearing a towel (or your swimming costume if the bath-house is mixed), you will be shown to a cubicle in the steamy marble washroom. Here, buckets of hot water will be poured over you, before you lie on a circular hot marble slab while an attendant (**tellak**) takes a coarse cloth to your skin to exfoliate. You'll finish off with a rinse and a massage.

hamam ha-mam	turkish baths
erkekler er-kek-ler	men
kadınlar ka-duhn-lar	women
sıcak suh-djak	hot
soğuk so-ook	cold
sabun sa-boon	soap

havlu hav-loo	towel
lif leef	loofah
takunya ta-koon-ya	bath clogs
kese ke-se	coarse rubbing-glove

Where are the baths?	**Hamam nerede?** ha-mam ne-re-de?
Where do I undress?	**Nerede soyunabilirim?** ne-re-de so-yoo-na-bee-lee-reem?
Is the hamam only for women or is it mixed?	**Kadınlar hamamı mı, kadın-erkek karışık mı?** ka-duhn-lar ha-ma-muh muh, ka-duhn er-kek ka-ruh-shuhk muh?
I would like a massage	**Masaj istiyorum** ma-sazh ees-tee-yo-room
Where is the steam room?	**Sauna nerede?** sa-oo-na ne-re-de?

Communications

Telephone and mobile

• •

If you plan to make international calls, a phonecard is the most convenient way of paying for them. To phone Turkey from the UK, the international code is 00 90 plus the Turkish area code (e.g. 232 for Izmir) followed by the number. To phone the UK from Turkey, dial 00 then 44, followed by the area code minus the initial zero, e.g. for central London 00-44-207-.... You can also use certain smartphone apps to make international calls by connecting to Wi-Fi.

telefon kartı te-le-fon kar-tuh	phonecard
telefon rehberi te-le-fon reh-be-ree	telephone directory
kod kod	dialling code
akıllı telefon a-kuhl-luh te-le-fon	smartphone
şarj aleti sharzh a-le-tee	charger

Alo
a-lo
Hello

Alo, ben...
a-lo, ben...
Hello, this is...

...ile konuşmak istiyorum
...i-le ko-noosh-mak ees-tee-yo-room
I would like to speak to...

Bir saniye
beer sa-nee-ye
Just a second

I want to make a phone call	**Telefon etmek istiyorum** te-le-fon et-mek ees-tee-yo-room
Where can I buy a phonecard?	**Nereden telefon kartı alabilirim?** ne-re-den te-le-fon kar-tuh a-la-bee-lee-reem?
Please write the phone number down	**Lütfen telefon numarasını yazın** lewt-fen te-le-fon noo-ma-ra-suh-nuh ya-zuhn
Can I speak to...	**...ile görüşebilir miyim** ...ee-le gur-rew-she-bee-leer mee-yeem
I'll call back later	**Sonra tekrar ararım** son-ra tek-rar a-ra-ruhm

Do you have a ... charger?	**Diz üstü ... şarj aletiniz var mı?** deez-oos-too sharzh a-le-tee-neez var-muh?
Can I borrow your...?	**...kullanabilir miyim?** ...koo-la-na-bee-leer-mee-yeem?
I have an e-ticket on my phone	**E-biletim telefonumda** e-bee-le-teem te-le-fo-nuhm-da
I need to phone a UK/US/Australian number	**Birleşik Krallık/Amerika/ Avustralya numarası aramam lâzım** beer-le-sheek kral-luhk/ a-me-ree-ka/a-voos-tral-ya noo-me-ra-suh a-ra-mam la-zuhm

YOU MAY HEAR...	
Alo?/Efendim? a-lo/e-fen-deem	Hello?
Lütfen bekleyin lewt-fen bek-le-yeen	Please hold on
Kim arıyordu? keem a-ruh-yor-dooh?	Who is calling?
Daha sonra arayabilir misiniz? da-ha son-ra a-ra-ya-bee-leer mee-see-neez?	Can you call back later?
Mesajınız var mı? me-sa-zhuh-nuhz var muh?	Do you want to leave a message?
Yanlış numara yan-luhsh noo-ma-ra	Wrong number

Text messaging

· · · · · · · · · · · · · · · · ·

I will text you	**Sana mesaj gönderirim**	
	sa-na me-sazh gurn-de-ree-reem	
Can you text me?	**Bana mesaj gönderebilir misin?**	
	ba-na me-sazh gurn-de-re-bee-leer mee-seen?	
text (message)	**mesaj**	
	me-sazh	
to send a text (message)	**mesaj göndermek**	
	me-sazh guhn-der-mek	

For texting in Turkish, some widely used abbreviations are:

slm	**selam**	hi
nbr?	**naber? (ne haber)**	what's up?
nsln?	**nasılsın?**	how are you?
tşk	**teşekkürler**	thanks
tmm	**tamam**	OK/fine
cnm	**canım**	my dear/love
bb	**bye bye**	bye
grşz	**görüşürüz**	see you
o pt	**öptüm**	kiss

E-mail

The internet suffix for Turkey is **.tr**.

My e-mail address is...	**E-mail adresim...** ee-meyl ad-re-seem...
What is your e-mail address?	**E-mail adresiniz nedir?** ee-meyl ad-re-see-neez ne-deer?
How do you spell it?	**Harf harf söyler misiniz?** harf harf sur-y-ler-mee-see-neez?
Can I send an e-mail?	**E-mail gönderebilir miyim?** ee-meyl gurn-de-re-bee-leer mee-yeem?
Did you get my e-mail?	**E-mailimi aldınız mı?** ee-mey-lee-mee al-duh-nuhz-muh?

Internet

ana sayfa an-a say-fa	home
kullanıcı adı kool-la-nuh-djuh a-duh	username
aramak a-ra-mak	to browse

parola/şifre pa-ro-la/sheef-re	password
uyg (short for **uygulama**) ooy (oo-la-ma)	app
diz üstü bilgisayar deez-oos-too beel-gee-sa-yar	laptop
sosyal medya sos-yal med-ya	social network
tablet/bloknot tab-let/blok-not	tablet
kablosuz bağlantı kab-lo-suz ba-lan-tuh	Wi-Fi

What is the Wi-Fi password?	**Kablosuz bağlantı şifresi nedir?** kab-lo-suhz ba-lan-tuh sheef-re-see ne-deer?
Do you have free Wi-Fi?	**Ücretsiz kablosuz/ Wi-fi bağlantı var mı?** ewj-ret-seez kab-lo-suz/ wi-fi ba-lan-tuh var muh?
Add me on Facebook	**Beni facebook'a ekle** be-nee fays-book-a ek-le
Is there a 3G/4G signal?	**3G/4G sinyali var mı?** ewch geh/durt geh seen-ya-lee var muh?

I need to access my webmail	**Web postama ulaşmam lâzım** veb pos-ta-ma oo-lash-mam la-zuhm
I would like to use Skype	**Skype kullanmak istiyorum** skype koo-lan-mak ees-tee-yo-room
I would like to print some pages	**Çıktı almak istiyorum** chuhk-tuh al-mak ees-tee-yo-rum

Practicalities

Money

Banking hours are Monday to Friday, 9 a.m. to 12 p.m. and 1.30 to 5 p.m. The best place to change money is at a **döviz bürosu** or bureau de change. If there are none around, jewellery shops are a good alternative. Also look out for the word **kambiyo**: these are generally found in tourist areas and are open long hours. The Turkish currency is **Türk Lirası (TL)**.

dollars	**dollar**	do-lar
exchange rate	**döviz kuru**	do-veez koo-roo
pounds	**Sterlin**	ster-lin

Where is the nearest bank?	**En yakın banka nerede?** en ya-kuhn ban-ka ne-re-de?	
Can I change money here?	**Döviz bozuyor musunuz?** duh-veez bo-zoo-yor moo-soo-nooz?	
I want to change £50	**Elli Sterlin bozdurmak istiyorum** el-lee ster-leen boz-door-mak ees-tee-yo-room	

What is the exchange rate for...?	**...karşılığı döviz kuru nedir?** ...kar-shuh-luh-uh do-veez koo-roo ne-deer?

Paying

. . . .

Credit cards are widely accepted. Service charges are included in restaurants, bars and cafés, but a 10% tip is customary.

hesap he-sap	bill
fiş feesh	receipt
fatura fa-too-ra	invoice
kasa ka-sa	cash desk
kredi kartı kre-dee kar-tuh	credit card
sadece nakit sa-de-je na-keet	cash only
para çekmek pa-ra chek-mek	to withdraw money
banka kartı (ATM kartı) ban-ka kar-tuh (ah-te-meh kar-tuh)	debit card

temassız ödeme te-ma-suhz uh-deh-me	contactless payment
POS cihazı pos djee-ha-zhuh	card payment machine

How much is it?	**Ne kadar?** ne ka-dar?
Can I pay by credit card?	**kredi kartı ile ödeyebilir miyim?** kre-dee kar-tuh ee-le ur-de-ye-bee-leer mee-yeem?
Where do I pay?	**Nereye ödeyeyim?** ne-re-ye ur-de-ye-yeem?
I'd like a receipt, please	**Fiş alabilir miyim?** feesh a-la-bee-leer mee-yeem?
I think there is a mistake	**Sanırım bir yanlışlık var** sa-nuh-ruhm beer yan-luhsh-luhk var
Keep the change	**Üstü kalsın** ews-tew kal-suhn
Can I pay in cash?	**Nakit ödeyebilir miyim?** na-keet uh-de-ye-bee-leer mee-yeem?
Where is the nearest cash machine?	**En yakın ATM nerede?** en ya-kuhn ah-te-me ne-re-de?
Is there a credit card charge?	**Kredi kartı ücreti var mı?** kre-dee kar-tuh ewj-re-tee var muh?

| Is there a discount for senior citizens? | **Yaşlılar için indirim var mı?** yash-luh-lar ee-cheen een-dee-reem var muh? |
| Can you write down the price? | **Fiyatı yazabilir misiniz?** fee-ya-tuh ya-za-bee-leer mee-see-neez? |

Luggage

bavul ba-vool	suitcase
el çantası el chan-ta-suh	handbag
evrak çantası ev-rak chan-ta-suh	briefcase
el bagajı el- ba-ga-zhuh	hand luggage
emanet bürosu e-ma-net bew-ro-soo	left-luggage office
kilitli emanet dolabı kee-leet-lee e-ma-net do-la-buh	locker
el arabası el a-ra-ba-suh	trolley

| My suitcase hasn't arrived | **Bavulum çıkmadı** ba-voo-loom chuhk-ma-duh |
| ...is missing | **...kayboldu** ...kay-bol-doo |

...is damaged	**...hasar görmüş** ...ha-sar gur-mewsh
Can I leave my suitcase here?	**Bavulumu burada bırakabilir miyim?** ba-voo-loo-moo boo-ra-da buh-ra-ka-bee-leer mee-yeem?
Is there a left-luggage office?	**Emanet bürosu var mı?** e-ma-net bew-ro-soo var muh?

Laundry

· ·

çamaşır deterjanı cha-ma-shuhr de-ter-zha-nuh	washing powder
kuru temizleyici koo-roo te-meez-le-yee-djee	dry-cleaner's

| Where can I wash some clothes? | **Çamaşır yıkayabileceğim bir yer var mı?**
cha-ma-shuhr yuh-ka-ya-bee-le-dje-eem beer yer var muh? |
| Where is the launderette? | **Çamaşırhane nerede?**
cha-ma-shuhr-ha-ne ne-re-de? |

Complaints

This doesn't work	**Bu çalışmıyor** boo cha-luhsh-muh-yor
The room is dirty	**Oda kirli** o-da keer-lee
The room is too hot/cold	**Oda çok sıcak/soğuk** o-da chok suh-djak/so-ook
I didn't order this	**Bunu ısmarlamadım** boo-noo uhs-mar-la-ma-duhm
I want to complain	**Şikayet etmek istiyorum** shee-ka-yet et-mek ees-tee-yo-room
Please call the manager	**Lütfen müdürü çağırın** lewt-fen mew-dew-rew cha-uh-ruhn
out of order	**bozuk** bo-zook
toilet	**tuvalet** tu-va-let
shower	**duş** dush

Problems

• •

Can you help me?	**Yardım edebilir misiniz?** yar-duhm e-de-bee-leer mee-see-neez?
I don't speak Turkish	**Türkçe bilmiyorum** tewrk-che beel-mee-yo-room
Do you speak English?	**İngilizce biliyor musunuz?** een-gee-leez-dje bee-lee-yor moo-soo-nooz?
I'm lost	**Kayboldum** kay-bol-doom
I need to go to...	**...gitmek istiyorum** ...geet-mek ees-tee-yo-room
the station	**İstasyona** ees-tas-yo-na
my hotel	**otelime** o-te-lee-me
this address	**bu adrese** boo ad-re-se
I've missed my train/bus/plane	**Trenimi/otobüsümü/ uçağımı kaçırdım** tre-nee-mee/o-to-bew-sew-mew/ oo-cha-uh-muh ka-chuhr-duhm
I've missed the connection	**Aktarmayı kaçırdım** ak-tar-ma-yuh ka-chuhr-duhm

87

The coach has left without me	**Otobüs beni almadan gitmiş** o-to-bews be-nee al-ma-dan geet-meesh
How does this work?	**Bu nasıl çalışıyor?** boo na-suhl cha-luh-shuh-yor?
I lost my money	**Paramı kaybettim** pa-ra-muh kay-bet-teem
I need to access my online banking	**İnternet banka hesabıma ulaşmam lâzım** een-ter-net ban-ka he-sa-buh-ma oo-lash-mam la-zuhm
This is broken	**Bu kırık** boo kuh-ruhk
Can you repair...?	**...tamir edebilir misiniz?** ...ta-meer e-de-bee-leer mee-see-neez?
How long will it take?	**Ne kadar sürer?** ne ka-dar sew-rer?

Emergencies

· ·

Emergency phone numbers in Turkey are as follows:

Police **155**
Fire brigade **110**
Medical emergency **113**
Coastguard **158**
Tourist police **0212 527 4503**

polis po-lees	police
itfaiye eet-fa-ee-ye	fire brigade
ambulans am-boo-lans	ambulance
hastane has-ta-ne	hospital
acil servis a-djeel ser-vees	A&E

Help!	**İmdat!** eem-dat!
Fire!	**Yangın!** yan-guhn!
There's been an accident	**Bir kaza oldu** beer ka-za ol-doo
Please help me	**Lütfen yardım edin** lewt-fen yar-duhm e-deen
Please call the police/ fire brigade/ ambulance/ doctor	**Lütfen polis/itfaiye/ ambulans/doktor çağırın** lewt-fen po-lees/eet-fa-ee-ye/ am-boo-lans/dok-tor cha-uh-ruhn
Someone has been injured	**Birisi yaralandı** bee-ree-see ya-ra-lan-duh
Where is the police station?	**Karakol nerede?** ka-ra-kol ne-re-de?
I've been robbed	**Soyuldum** so-yool-doom
I've been raped	**Tecavüze uğradım** te-dja-vew-ze oo-ra-duhm

I want to speak to a policewoman	**Bir bayan polisle konuşmak istiyorum** beer ba-yan po-lees-le ko-noosh-mak ees-tee-yo-room
Someone has stolen...	**Birisi ... çaldı** bee-ree-see ... chal-duh
I've lost...	**...kaybettim** ...kay-bet-teem
my money	**Paramı** pa-ra-muh
my passport	**Pasaportumu** pa-sa-por-too-moo
My son is missing	**Oğlum kayboldu** o-loom kay-bol-doo
My daughter is missing	**Kızım kayboldu** kuh-zuhm kay-bol-doo
His/Her name is...	**Adı...** a-duh...
I need a report for my insurance	**Sigortam için rapor almam lazım** see-gor-tam ee-cheen ra-por al-mam la-zuhm

Health

Pharmacy

. . . .

Pharmacies (**eczane**) keep the same hours as other shops. The night duty pharmacy is **nöbetçi eczane.** Pharmacists may be able to dispense medicines which would normally only be available on prescription in the UK. In south and south west Turkey, there is often a mosquito problem during summer. Tourist areas are usually sprayed before the high season and mosquito repellents are available in all pharmacies.

Where is the nearest pharmacy?	**En yakın eczane nerede?** en ya-kuhn edj-za-ne ne-re-de?
I need something...	**...bir şey istiyorum** ...beer shey ees-tee-yo-room
for diarrhoea	**ishal için** ees-hal ee-cheen
for constipation	**kabızlık için** ka-buhz-luhk ee-cheen
for food poisoning	**gıda zehirlenmesi için** guh-da ze-heer-len-me-see ee-cheen

Is it safe for...?	**...için güvenli mi?**
	...ee-cheen gew-ven-lee mee?
children	**çocuklar**
	cho-djook-lar
I am pregnant	**hamileyim**
	ha-mee-le-yeem
What is the dose?	**Ne kadar alınacak?**
	ne ka-dar a-luh-na-djak?

YOU MAY HEAR...

Günde üç kere gewn-de ewch ke-re	3 times a day
yemeklerden önce/sonra ye-mek-ler-den urn-dje/son-ra	before/after food
yemekle beraber ye-mek-le be-ra-ber	with food

asthma	**astım**	as-tuhm
condom	**prezervatif**	pre-zer-va-teef
contact lenses	**kontak lens**	kon-tak lens
inhaler	**soluk rahatma cihazı/soluk rahatlatma spreyi**	so-luhk ra-hat-ma djee-ha-zuh/so-luhk ra-hat-lat-ma spray-ee
morning-after pill	**ertesi gün hapı**	er-te-see goon ha-puh

Health

92

mosquito bite	**sivrisinek sokması**	seev-ree-see-nek sok-ma-suh
mosquito repellent	**sivrisinek kovucu**	seev-ree-see-nek ko-vuh-djuh
painkillers	**ağrı kesici**	ah-ruh ke-see-jee
period	**adet**	a-det
the Pill	**doğum kontrol hapı**	do-oom kon-trol ha-puh
tampon	**tampon**	tam-pon

Body

· ·

I have broken...	**...kırdım** ...kuhr-duhm
my foot	**ayağımı** a-ya-uh-muh
my ankle	**bileğimi** bee-le-ee-mee
It hurts	**Ağrıyor** a-ruh-yor

arm	**kol**	kol
back	**sırt**	suhrt
chest	**göğüs**	guh-huz

93

ear	**kulak**	koo-lak
eye	**göz**	guhz
foot	**ayak**	a-yak
head	**baş**	bash
heart	**kalp**	kalp
leg	**bacak**	ba-jak
neck	**boyun**	bo-yun
toe	**ayak parmağı**	a-yak par-ma-uh
tooth	**diş**	deesh
wrist	**bilek**	bee-lek

Doctor

hastane has-ta-ne	hospital
acil servis a-djeel ser-vees	A&E
reçete re-che-te	prescription
ambulans am-boo-lans	ambulance

Kendimi iyi hissetmiyorum
ken-dee-mee ee-yee hees-set-mee-yo-room
I don't feel right

Ateşiniz var mı?
a-te-shee-neez var muh?
Do you have a temperature?

Hayır/Evet. Buram ağrıyor
ha-yuhr/e-vet. boo-ram a-ruh-yor
No/Yes. I have a pain here

I need to see a doctor	**Doktora görünmem gerek** dok-to-ra gur-rewn-mem ge-rek
My son/daughter is ill	**Oğlum/Kızım hasta** o-loom/kuh-zuhm has-ta
I'm on the Pill	**Doğum kontrol hapı alıyorum** do-oom kon-trol ha-puh a-luh-yo-room
I'm diabetic	**şeker hastasıyım** she-ker has-ta-suh-yuhm
I need insulin	**İnsülin almam lazım** een-sew-leen al-mam la-zuhm
I'm allergic to pollen/dairy/gluten/nuts/penicillin	**Polene/süt ürünlere/glutene/fıstığa/penisiline alerjim var** po-le-ne/soot oo-roon-ler-e/gloo-te-ne/fuhs-tuh-a a-ler-jeem/pe-nee-see-lee-ne var

Health

95

I have a prescription for...	**...için reçetem var** ...ee-cheen re-che-tem var
I've run out of medication	**İlacım bitti** ee-la-juhm beet-tee
epilepsy	**sara** sa-ra
STI or STD (sexually transmitted infection/disease)	**cinsel yolla bulaşan hastalık/enfeksiyon** jeen-sel yol-la buh-luh-shan has-ta-luhk/en-fek-si-yon
food poisoning	**gıda zehirlenmesi** guh-da ze-heer-len-me-see
headache	**baş ağrısı** bash-ah-ruh-suh
drug abuse	**uyuşturucu kullanmak** oo-yoosh-too-roo-joo kool-lan-mak
sprain	**incitmek** een-jeet-mek
GP (general practitioner)	**aile doktoru** ay-le dok-to-ruh
A&E (accident and emergency)	**acil servis** a-jeel sehr-vis
Can you give me a receipt for the insurance?	**Sigorta şirketi için fiş verir misiniz?** si-gor-taa sheer-ke-tee ee-cheen feesh ve-reer-mee-see-neez?

Alkol kullanmayınız al-kol koo-lan-ma-yuh-nuhz	Do not drink alcohol
İçki içiyor musunuz? eech-kee ee-chee-yor moo-soo-nooz?	Do you drink?
Sigara içiyor musunuz? see-ga-ra ee-chee-yor moo-soo-nooz?	Do you smoke?
Uyuşturucu kullanıyor musunuz? oo-yoosh-too-roo-joo koo-la-nuh-yor moo-soo-nuhz?	Do you take drugs?

Health

Dentist

. . . .

You will have to pay for dental treatment on the
spot, so make sure you get a receipt to be able to
claim a refund from your holiday insurance.

dolgu dol-goo	filling
köprü kurp-rew	crown
protez pro-tez	dentures
iğne ee-ne	injection

97

I need to go to a dentist	**Dişçiye gitmem gerek** deesh-chee-ye geet-mem ge-rek
He/she has toothache	**Dişi ağrıyor** dee-shee a-ruh-yor
This hurts	**Burası ağrıyor** boo-ra-suh a-ruh-yor
Can you do emergency treatment?	**Acil tedavi yapabilir misiniz?** a-djeel te-da-vee ya-pa-bee-leer mee-see-neez?

Eating out

Eating places

Büfe Snack bar or street stall selling sandwiches and pastries.

Dürümcü Small kebab shop.

Pideci Serves pitta-like bread with a variety of toppings. Turkish equivalent of a pizzeria.

Meyhane Traditional taverna.

Şarapevi Wine bar serving a variety of traditional and European food.

Pastane Cake shop serving cakes, pastries and soft drinks.

Restoran Licensed restaurant with waiter service. Although lunch is normally served from 12 to 2 p.m. and dinner from 7 to 10 p.m., restaurants in Turkey will usually serve food outside these times as well.

Lokanta More modest type of restaurant, usually not serving alcohol.

Hazır yemek Serves a selection of ready-made dishes.

Kebapçı Serves shish and doner kebabs.

Köfteci Serves kebabs, meatballs and other grilled dishes.

Ocakbaşı Specialised meat restaurant with an open charcoal fire by which you can sit and cook your own food.

Piknik yeri/alanı Picnic area.

In a bar/café

Tea (çay) is served Turkish-style in little tulip-shaped glasses with no milk. A pleasant variation is apple tea (elma çayı). Turkish coffee (kahve) is served very strong, black, and either without sugar, medium or sweet; so when you order coffee you will always be asked how you prefer it. Try not to drain your cup, as the coffee is not filtered and the dregs will be at the bottom. Cappuccino, espresso and instant coffee are also available.

Sparkling mineral water (maden suyu) and cold soft drinks can be found at most establishments. Ayran is a sharp, refreshing drink made by diluting yoghurt with water & salt.

Although Turkey is a Muslim country, alcoholic drinks are widely available. The national alcoholic drink is rakı, a strong aniseed-flavoured spirit, usually mixed with water and served with ice. Locally produced wines **Doluca**, **Kavaklıdere** and **Çankaya** are also good.

FACE TO FACE

Ne arzu edersiniz?
Ne ar-zoo e-der-see-neez?
What would you like?

Sütlü bir çay lütfen
sewt-lew beer chay lewt-fen
A tea with milk please

A ... please	**Bir ... lütfen** beer ... lewt-fen
2 ... please	**İki ... lütfen** ee-kee ... lewt-fen
Do you have...?	**...var mı?** ...var muh?
Do you have beer?	**Bira var mı?** bee-ra var muh?
A bottle of sparkling water	**Bir şişe maden suyu** beer shee-she ma-den soo-yoo
mineral water (still)	**şişe suyu** shee-she soo-yoo
A cappuccino, please	**Bir kapuçino, lütfen** beer ka-poo-chee-no, lewt-fen
A tea, please	**Bir çay, lütfen** beer chay, lewt-fen

with milk	**sütlü**
	sewt-lew
with lemon	**limonlu**
	lee-mon-loo
with ice	**buzlu**
	booz-loo
with sugar	**şekerli**
	she-ker-lee
One more, please	**Bir tane daha, lütfen**
	beer ta-ne da-ha, lewt-fen

Although tap water is safe to drink, it contains high amounts of chloride and many people prefer to drink bottled water.

Reading the menu

. . . .

There are eating places everywhere, usually open from early morning until late at night. If you were planning to eat a full Turkish meal, you would begin with **soğuk meze** (cold starters), followed by **sıcak meze** (hot starters) and **ana yemek** (main course), and end with **fruit** (meyve) or **tatlı** (dessert). Dinner is a very sociable occasion in Turkey: people often sit and talk for hours.

| The menu, please | **Menü, lütfen** |
| | me-new, lewt-fen |

Do you have a children's menu?	**Çocuk menusu var mı?** cho-djook me-new-sew var muh?
What is this?	**Bu nedir?** boo ne-deer?
I'd like this	**Bundan alayım** boon-dan a-la-yuhm
What is the speciality of the house?	**Spesiyaliteniz nedir?** spe-see-ya-lee-te-neez ne-deer?
Excuse me!	**Afedersiniz!** a-fe-der-see-neez!
The bill, please	**Hesap, lütfen** he-sap, lewt-fen
Some more bread/water, please	**Biraz daha ekmek/su, lütfen** bee-raz da-ha ek-mek/soo, lewt-fen
a high chair	**mama sandalyesi** ma-ma san-dal-ye-see
Another glass, please	**Bir bardak daha, lütfen** beer bar-dak da-ha, lewt-fen
homemade	**ev yapımı** ev ya-puh-muh
local delicacy	**yerel lezzetler** ye-rel lez-zet-ler

In a restaurant

Although splitting the bill is the norm nowadays, traditional Turkish etiquette dictates that the host – the person who invites – should pay the bill. It is always polite to offer to share the bill, but insisting too much may be considered offensive. Remember, Muslims do not eat pork (**domuz eti**); to ask for it may be impolite. Only restaurants in tourist destinations will serve pork. All meat in Turkey is halal.

Is there a set menu?	**Set menü var mı?**	set me-noo var muh?
We would like a table for ... people, please	**...kişilik bir masa, lütfen**	...kee-shee-leek beer ma-sa, lewt-fen
This isn't what I ordered	**Ismarladığım bu değil**	uhs-mar-la-duh-uhm boo de-eel
The ... is too...	**...çok...**	...chok...

cold	**soğuk**	so-uhk
greasy	**yağlı**	yah-luh
rare	**az pişmiş**	az peesh-meesh
salty	**tuzlu**	tuz-loo
spicy	**acılı, baharatlı**	a-juh-luh, ba-ha-rat-luh

| warm | ılık | uh-luk |
| well cooked | iyi pişmiş | ee-yee peesh-meesh |

Common dishes

arnavut ciğeri pan-fried lamb's liver, served with onion salad

çoban salata cubed tomatoes, green pepper and cucumber, dressed with parsley and seasoning

fava boiled broad beans marinated with onions and parsley, served with olive oil and lemon juice

hoşafı fruit stewed in sweet juice

izmir köfte meatballs cooked in the oven with potatoes, green pepper and tomatoes, served with rice

kısır cracked wheat salad with tomato, onion, parsley, green pepper, lemon juice and olive oil

sigara böreği filo rolls with feta cheese and parsley

Snacks (hafif yemek)

börek crispy filo pastry, filled with cheese, spinach or mince

çerez selection of nuts, raisins, bar nibbles

lahmacun round and flat Turkish pizza with mince, onion, tomatoes and peppers

muska böreği amulet-shaped filo parcel filled with mince

pide pitta bread with different toppings (cheese, mince, meat cubes, salami etc.)

Appetizers (meze)

arnavut ciğeri deep-fried cubes of lamb's liver served with onion salad

cacık yoghurt with cucumber and garlic

humus chickpea dip with tahini and garlic

İmam bayıldı aubergines stuffed with tomatoes, green pepper and onion

midye dolma mussels stuffed with rice, pine kernels and currants

midye tava fried mussels

patlıcan salatası aubergine salad

Rus salatası 'Russian salad' (diced vegetables in mayonnaise)

tarama taramasalata (fish-roe purée)

yaprak dolması stuffed vine leaves

yoğurtlu bakla broad beans with yoghurt

zeytin olives

Side dishes

Most things are eaten with rice, though chips are usually available.

patates kızartması chips

pide pitta bread

pilav rice

sebze vegetables

turşu pickled vegetables

Kebabs (kebap)

çöp kebap several skewers of small pieces of lamb

döner kebap slices of spit-roasted lamb in pitta bread

kağıt kebap meat cooked in paper

patlıcan kebap meat with fried aubergine

saç kebap stir-fried lamb and vegetables

şiş kebap large chunks of lamb on a skewer with onions, tomatoes and peppers, eaten with rice

tavuk şiş chicken version of **şiş kebap**

Desserts (tatilar)

Turkey is famous for its very sweet desserts, but fruit is also popular.

aşure pudding made of wheat, nuts and dried fruit, known as Noah's pudding

ayva tatlısı sweet quinces served with cream

baklava filo pastry with chopped walnuts or pistachios, in syrup

kadayıf shredded pastry stuffed with nuts, served in syrup

kazandibi caramelised milk pudding

keşkül almond custard, served with almonds, pistachios and pomegranate seeds

lokma fritter balls in syrup, Turkish equivalent of the doughnut!

muhallebi milk pudding

sütlaç rice-pudding

şekerpare almond pastries in syrup

Dietary requirements

There are no specialist vegetarian restaurants, but in all restaurants most of the cold starters and some of the hot starters (**meze**) are vegetarian. Turkish people love light vegetarian dishes, especially during the summer.

I am vegetarian	**Vejetaryenim** ve-zhe-tar-ye-neem
I have a ... allergy	**...alerjim var** ...a-ler-jeem var
Is it ...-free?	**...siz mi?** ...seez mee?
I don't eat...	**...eti yemiyorum** ...e-tee ye-mee-yo-room

coeliac	**çölyak**	chuhl-yak
dairy	**süt ürünler**	soot oo-roon-ler
gluten	**gluten**	gloo-ten
nuts	**fıstık**	fuhs-tuk
organic	**organik**	or-ga-nik
vegan	**vegan**	ve-gan
wheat	**buğday**	boo-dai

Wines and spirits

· ·

Although Turkey is a Muslim country you can get alcoholic drinks including Turkish wines and beer. **Rakı** (similar to Greek Ouzo) is usually drunk with **meze**, a selection of appetizers. In towns, especially in Anatolia and the south east, many restaurants don't serve alcohol during the fasting month of Ramadan.

The wine list, please	**Şarap listesi, lütfen** sha-rap lees-te-see, lewt-fen
Can you recommend a good wine?	**İyi bir şarap önerir misiniz?** ee-yee beer sha-rap ur-ne-reer mee-see-neez?
A bottle of...	**Bir şişe...** beer shee-she...
red wine	**kırmızı şarap** kuhr-muh-zuh sha-rap

rosé wine	**pembe şarap**	
	pem-be sha-rap	
white wine	**beyaz şarap**	
	be-yaz sha-rap	
A glass of...	**Bir bardak...**	
	beer bar-dak...	
a dry wine	**sek şarap**	
	sek sha-rap	
a local wine	**yerel şarap**	
	ye-rel sha-rap	
a sweet wine	**tatlı şarap**	
	tat-luh sha-rap	
What liqueurs do you have?	**Hangi likörler var?**	
	han-gee lee-kur-ler var?	

If your host is religious, it may be a good idea to observe the other guests before ordering alcohol. In some religious families, younger members of the family also don't drink alcohol in the presence of their elders.

Menu reader

acı bitter, hot, spicy

acıbiber hot chillies

acılı ezme spicy tomato salad with fresh herbs

açık çay weak tea

açma croissant-type round pastry

adaçayı sage tea

adana kebap spicy meat balls grilled on skewers

alabalık ızgarası grilled trout

alkollü içkiler alcoholic drinks, spirits

alkolsüz içkiler soft drinks

amerikan salatası salad with boiled peas, carrot and potatoes in mayonnaise sauce

ana yemek main course

ara sıcak light warm dishes served between cold starters and main course

armut hoşafı stewed pear in sweet juice

arnavut ciğeri fried liver served with onions and herbs

aşure traditional dessert made with wheat grains, nuts and dried fruits

ayran drink made of yoghurt and water, served chilled

ayva reçeli quince jam

ayva tatlısı quince dessert with fresh cream

az pişmiş cooked rare

az şekerli kahve slightly sweetened Turkish coffee

badem ezmesi marzipan

badem kurabiyesi almond cookies

baharat spices

bahçıvan kebabı baked meat and vegetables

bakla broad beans

baklava flaky pastry with nuts in syrup (dessert)

balık çeşitleri fish dishes

balık çorbası fish soup

barbunya borlotti beans

barbunya pilaki borlotti beans cooked in tomato and olive oil sauce

beğendi baked, mashed aubergine with béchamel sauce, served with lamb or meatballs in tomato sauce

beyaz peynir white cheese (feta-type but usually made of sheep's milk)

beyaz peynirli makarna pasta with white cheese

beyin salatası lambs' brain salad

beyti kebap grilled mince meat wrapped in flat bread and served with yoghurt and tomato sauce

bezelye çorbası pea soup

biber dolması stuffed green peppers

bitki çayı herbal tea

bonfile fillet steak, sirloin steak

börek filo parcels with cheese, meat or spinach

börülce black-eyed beans

buğulama steamed, poached

bulgur pilavı pilaf made with cracked wheat (bulgur)

burma kadayıf shredded and twisted pastry with nuts in syrup (dessert)

but leg, thigh (of meat)

buzlu with ice

buzlu badem fresh almonds served with ice

bülbül yuvası rounded flaky pastries with nuts in syrup (dessert)

cacık chopped cucumber in yoghurt flavoured with garlic and mint or dill

cevizli kek walnut cake

cevizli kurabiye walnut cookies

cezerye sweets made of caramelised and mashed carrots and nuts

cız-bız grilled, barbecued

ciğer ezme liver paste (pâté)

ciğer ızgara grilled liver

ciğer sote sautéed liver

ciğer tava pan-fried liver

cintonik gin and tonic

çamsakızı pine resin

çavdar ekmeği rye bread

çemen cumin paste

çerez mixture of nuts

çerkez tavuğu chicken in walnut and garlic sauce

çeşitli various, assorted

çılbır poached eggs served with garlic-flavoured yoghurt and paprika

çiğ (pişmemiş) raw, not cooked

çiğ börek pan-fried pasty with mince filling

çiğ köfte raw meatballs made with fine cracked-wheat, various hot chilli powders and other spices

çikolatalı dondurma chocolate ice cream

çikolatalı pasta chocolate cake

çilekli dondurma strawberry ice cream

çinekop small type of bluefish

çiroz salted dried mackerel

çoban kavurma lamb pieces fried in a Turkish wok with onion, peppers, tomatoes, garlic and herbs

çoban salatası a salad of chopped tomatoes, cucumber, peppers, onion and parsley

çok many, much

çok pişmiş well cooked

çöp kebabı (çöp şiş) small pieces of lamb grilled on wooden skewers

çörekotu black cumin seeds

dalyan köfte meatloaf with peas, boiled egg, and cubed potatoes; cooked in tomato sauce

dana rosto roast veal

demli çay strong tea

deniz ürünleri seafood dishes

deniz ürünleri salatası seafood salad

dil ox tongue

dilber dudağı lip-shaped cakes with nuts in syrup (dessert)

dilim slice

dolma stuffed vegetables (with or without meat)

domates çorbası tomato soup

domates dolması stuffed tomatoes

domatesli with tomatoes

domatesli pilav rice with tomatoes

domatesli pirinç çorbası rice soup with tomatoes

domates salatası tomato salad

domates salçası tomato paste

domates soslu in tomato sauce

ekmek kadayıfı pastry in syrup served with clotted cream (dessert)

ekşi sour

ekşili köfte (terbiyeli köfte) minced meat and rice balls in lemon and egg sauce

elbasan tava oven-baked lamb chops with yoghurt sauce

elma çayı apple tea

enginar dolması stuffed artichokes

erişte homemade pasta

etli with meat

etli bamya okra cooked with meat

etli bezelye peas cooked with meat

etli biber dolması peppers stuffed with mince and rice

etli bulgur pilavı cracked-wheat (bulgur) with meat

etli domates dolması tomatoes stuffed with mince and rice

etli kabak dolması courgettes stuffed with mince and rice

etli kapuska cabbage stew with meat

etli kuru fasulye white beans cooked with meat in tomato sauce

etli lahana dolması cabbage leaves stuffed with rice and meat

etli nohut chickpeas cooked with meat in tomato sauce

etli pilav rice cooked with meat

etli yaprak dolması (etli sarma) vine leaves stuffed with mince meat and rice

et suyu meat stock

ezme purée, mash, paste

ezogelin çorbası red lentil and rice soup

fasulye pilaki white beans cooked in olive oil and served cold

fasulye piyazı white bean and onion salad

fava broad bean pâté

fıçı bira draught beer

fırın oven, bakery

fırında baked, oven-roasted

fırında makarna oven-baked pasta

fırın muhallebi baked rice-flour pudding

fırın sütlaç baked rice pudding

fıstıklı with pistachio nuts

fıstıklı dondurma ice cream with pistachio nuts

füme smoked

galeta unu bread crumbs

garnitür garnish, trimmings, greens

gofret wafer

gözleme flat pastry with meat, cheese, spinach or jam filling, cooked on a griddle (like crêpes)

güllaç thin rice pastry layers with nuts in sweetened and rose-flavoured milk (dessert)

güveç, güveçte baked in earthenware cooking pot, casseroled

güveçte türlü casseroled meat and vegetables

hamsi very small and oily Black Sea sardines

hamsi buğulama steamed Black Sea sardines

hamsi kuşu fried sardines filled with herbs

hamsili pilav rice with sardines

hamsi tava pan-fried sardines

hamur işleri dishes made of dough (pasties/pastries)

hamur tatlıları pastry desserts

hanım göbeği 'lady's belly button'-shaped cakes in syrup

haşlama boiled, steamed, stewed

haşlama et stewed meat

haşlanmış yumurta hard-boiled egg

havuç dilimi carrot-shaped flaky pastry with nuts in syrup (dessert)

havuç kızartma fried carrot slices

havuç salatası carrot salad

haydari side dish with garlic-flavoured yoghurt and herbs

helva halva, sweets made of tahini, sugar and nuts

hindi dolması stuffed turkey

hoşaf stewed fruit in syrup, compote

humus garlic-flavoured chickpea purée with sesame oil

hünkar beğendi lamb served with baked aubergine purée

ıhlamur çayı linden-blossom tea

ıspanaklı börek pasties with spinach filling

ıspanaklı krep pancakes with spinach filling

ıspanaklı yumurta spinach omelette

ıspanak yemeği spinach cooked with meat in onion and tomato sauce

ızgara grilled, barbecued

içecek beverages, drinks

içki alcoholic drinks

içli köfte cracked-wheat balls stuffed with mince meat, onions, currants and pine nuts

iç pilav rice with currants, pine nuts, onions and fresh herbs

imam bayıldı aubergines filled with tomatoes, peppers and onions, cooked in olive oil and served cold

incir figs

irmik helvası dessert made of semolina, butter, sugar and pine nuts

iskender kebap (bursa iskender) special doner kebab served on pitta bread, in yoghurt, tomato and butter sauce

islim kebabı steamed kebab, diced lamb with fried aubergines, green peppers and tomatoes

istavrit horse mackerel

işkembe çorbası tripe soup

iyi pişmiş well cooked, well done

izmir köfte meatballs baked in tomato sauce with potatoes and green pepper slices

kabak courgettes, pumpkin, marrows

kabak dolması stuffed courgettes

kabak kızartması fried courgette slices

kabak oturtma courgettes cooked with meat, tomatoes and fresh herbs

kabak tatlısı pumpkin slices cooked in syrup (dessert)

kaburga ribs

kadayıf shredded and baked filo pastry filled with nuts, in syrup (dessert)

kadınbudu köfte fried meatballs with rice in egg and flour coating

kağıthelva disk-shaped wafers

kağıt kebabı lamb and vegetables baked in paper

kakaolu süt chocolate milk

kalburabastı semolina cakes in syrup, filled with walnut pieces

kalkan tava grilled turbot

kanat ızgara grilled chicken wings

kapuska cabbage stew with mince, onion, rice and parsley

karadut black mulberries

karagöz black bream

karides güveç casseroled shrimps

karışık mixed, assorted

karışık hoşaf assorted stewed fruits in syrup

karışık ızgara selection of grilled meats

karışık kızartma pan-fried mixed vegetables

karnıyarık aubergines filled with mince, onion, tomato, green pepper and garlic

kaşarlı köfte meatballs with mild cheese

kaşarlı pide pitta bread with mild cheese filling

kaşar peyniri cheddar-like mild cheese

katı (sert) hard, tough

katı yumurta hard-boiled egg

kavurma fried cubes of lamb (in their own fat)

kayısı hoşafı stewed apricots in syrup

kayısı reçeli apricot jam

kayısı suyu apricot juice

kaymak clotted cream (like mascarpone)

kaymaklı with clotted cream

kaymaklı dondurma plain ice cream

kazandibi oven-baked thick, milky pudding with a caramel base

kebap kebab, grilled/barbecued meat

kefal grey mullet

kelle boiled or grilled sheep's head

kelle-paça çorbası soup made of sheep's head and feet

kemalpaşa tatlısı round cakes in syrup (dessert)

kepek ekmeği bran bread

kestane şekeri sweet chestnuts cooked in syrup

keşkek mashed wheat cooked with lamb very slowly for a long time

keşkül milk pudding with almonds

kılıç ızgara grilled swordfish

kılıç şiş swordfish chunks grilled on skewers

kırmızı biber ground chilli pepper

kırmızı mercimek çorbası red lentil soup

kısır cracked-wheat salad with vegetables and fresh herbs

kış türlüsü stewed winter vegetables

kıymalı with minced meat

kıymalı bamya okra with minced meat

kıymalı ıspanak spinach with minced meat

kıymalı karnabahar cauliflower with minced meat

kıymalı makarna pasta or noodles with minced meat

kıymalı mercimek lentils with minced meat

kıymalı pide pitta bread with mince filling

kıymalı yumurta fried eggs with minced meat

kızartma fried

kızılcık cornelian cherry

kokoreç lamb's intestines grilled on a spit

komposto compote, general name for stewed fruits served cold in syrup

köfte meatballs

kömür ızgara grilled on a charcoal fire, barbecued

köpüklü şarap sparkling wine

köz (közlenmiş) grilled on ashes

kremalı pasta cream cake

krem karamel crème caramel

kremşanti whipped cream

krep pancake, crêpe

kumpir baked potato with various fillings

kurabiye cookies, small cakes

kuru dry, dried

kuru bakla dried broad beans

kuru fasulye white beans in tomato sauce

kuru incir dried figs

kuru kayısı dried apricot

kuru köfte fried meatballs

kuru yemiş general name for nuts and dried fruits

kuskus couscous

kuşbaşı small pieces of meat

kuşbaşılı pide pitta bread with small pieces of meat filling

kuyu kebap/kuyu tandır lamb baked in special wood-burning ovens

kuzu fırın roast lamb

kuzu haşlama stewed lamb

kuzu pirzola grilled lamb chops

kuzu tandır lamb baked in special ovens

külbastı lamb fillets grilled with herbs

lahana dolması stuffed cabbage leaves

lahana turşusu pickled cabbage

lahmacun pizza-like pitta with spicy meat topping

lakerda salted and pickled tunny

lavaş tortilla-like unleavened bread

leblebi roasted chickpeas

limonata drink made with lemon juice and sugar, served chilled

lokma tatlısı round pastries fried and served in syrup, Turkish doughnut

lokum Turkish Delight

lüfer blue fish

lüfer ızgara grilled blue fish

mantar çorbası mushroom soup

mantar ızgara grilled mushrooms

mantarlı et sote mushrooms sautéed with meat and vegetables

mantı Turkish ravioli with mince filling, served with garlic-flavoured yoghurt and pepper sauce

memba suyu spring water

menemen omelette with onions, tomatoes and peppers

mercan ızgara grilled bream

mercimek çorbası lentil soup

mercimek köftesi lentil croquettes mixed with fresh herbs

meşrubat soft drinks, beverages

mevsim salatası seasonal salad

meyve salatası fruit salad

meze small side dishes served cold as starters, appetizers

mezgit whiting

mısır ekmeği corn bread

mısır unu corn flour

midye dolması mussels stuffed with rice, pine kernels and currants

midyeli pilav rice with mussels

midye tava fried mussels

muhallebi rice-flour pudding

musakka moussaka

mutfak kitchen, cuisine

muzlu süt banana milkshake

mücver fritters of courgette, onion and fresh herbs

nar ekşisi (nar ekşili) pomegranate sour sauce

Nescafé® instant coffee

nohutlu pilav rice with chickpeas

nohutlu yahni chickpeas cooked with lamb

nohut yemeği chickpeas cooked in tomato sauce

ocakbaşı general name for restaurants where meat dishes are barbecued on an open charcoal fire

odun ateşi (odun fırını) wood-fired ovens

omlet omelette

ordövr tabağı starter platter (hors d'œuvres)

orman kebabı lamb cooked with vegetables and herbs

orta pişmiş medium cooked

orta şekerli kahve medium-sweet Turkish coffee

paça çorbası soup made with lamb's trotters

paçanga böreği filo parcel with pastrami and cheese filling

palamut bonito

palamut ızgara grilled bonito

pancar salatası beetroot salad

pancar turşusu pickled beetroot

papatya çayı camomile tea

paskalya çöreği easter bun– slightly sweetened bread in a plait

pastane pastry shop

pastırma pastrami, garlic and cumin-coated, cured beef

pastırmalı kuru fasulye white beans cooked with pastrami in tomato sauce

pastırmalı pide pitta bread baked with pastrami filling

patates köftesi fried potato croquettes

patatesli with potato

patates püresi mashed potato

patates salatası potato salad

patlıcan dolması stuffed aubergines

patlıcan dolma turşusu pickled stuffed aubergines

patlıcan kebap roasted aubergine and meat

patlıcan kızartması fried aubergines

patlıcan salatası aubergine purée

pavurya hermit crab, cray fish

pazı dolması stuffed chard leaves

pekmez grape molasses

pestil pressed and dried fruit pulp

peynirli with cheese

peynirli börek pastry layers with cheese filling

peynirli omlet cheese omelette

peynirli pide pitta-like bread with cheese topping

pide pitta-like bread with various fillings, baked in a wood-fired oven

pilaki white beans and vegetables in tomato sauce and olive oil

pilav cooked rice

piliç bonfile grilled chicken breast

piliç ızgara grilled chicken

piliç kanat grilled chicken wings

piliç pirzola grilled chicken thighs

piliç şiş chicken pieces grilled on skewers

pirinç rice (uncooked)

pirinç çorbası rice soup

pirzola lamb chops/cutlets

pişmaniye kind of flaky **halva** made of sugar, butter and flour

pişmemiş uncooked

piyaz white bean salad

poğaça pastry parcels with meat or cheese filling

porsiyon portion

portakal reçeli orange jam

poşet çay tea-bags

puf böreği filo parcels with meat or cheese filling

püre purée, mash

rafadan medium-boiled egg

rakı aniseed-flavoured spirit (similar to ouzo)

rendelenmiş grated

revani semolina cake with syrup

roka kind of watercress, rocket

rosto slices of roast meat served with tomato sauce

rozbif roast beef

126 **rulo köfte** roll-shaped meatloaf

rus salatası (amerikan salatası) salad made with boiled peas, carrots, potatos in mayonnaise sauce

saç flat iron cooking pan, Turkish wok

saç kavurma lamb pieces fried on a griddle

sade kahve Turkish coffee without sugar

sade Nescafé® black instant coffee

sade pilav plain rice (pilaf)

sahanda yumurta fried eggs

sahan köftesi pan-fried meatballs

sahlep (salep) hot drink made of **salep** (powder made from dried orchids), milk and sugar, served with cinnamon powder

sakatat offal

salam salami

salamura cured in brine

salça tomato paste

salçalı köfte meat balls in tomato sauce

sandviç sandwiches, bread rolls with various fillings

sarımsaklı with garlic

sarımsaklı yoğurt yoghurt with garlic

sazan balığı carp

sebze çorbası vegetable soup

sebzeli köfte meatballs cooked with vegetables

sebzeli tavuk casseroled chicken with vegetables

sek dry, straight drink

sek rakı raki without water, neat **raki**

sek şarap dry wine

semizotu purslane

sert hard, strong, tough

sıcak hot, warm

sıcak yemekler hot dishes

sigara böreği cigarette-shaped filo parcels with mince or cheese and parsley filling

simit ring-shaped rolls covered with sesame seeds, Turkish bagel

sivri biber green hot peppers

soğan dolması stuffed onions

soğan yahni casseroled small onions with lamb

soğuk cold, cool, chilled

soğuk yemekler cold dishes

somon füme smoked salmon

sosis sausage, frankfurter

soslu in sauce

söğüş cold cuts of meat

su böreği moist filo layers baked in the oven with cheese and parsley filling

sucuk ekmek bread rolls with grilled Turkish sausage

sucuklu Turkish sausage with garlic and spices

sucuklu pide pitta bread with Turkish sausage filling

sucuklu yumurta fried eggs with Turkish sausage

sulu köfte meatball soup

sulu yemek dishes cooked in sauces

sumak sumac (a lemony, tangy spice)

su muhallebisi rice-flour pudding sprinkled with rose water

supangle chocolate pudding

sütlaç rice pudding

sütlü with milk

sütlü kahve coffee with milk

sütlü tatlılar milky desserts, puddings

süzme mercimek çorbası strained red lentil soup

süzme yoğurt strained yoghurt

şeftali reçeli peach jam

şeftali suyu peach juice

şehriye fine noodle

şehriyeli pilav rice with fine noodles

şehriyeli tavuk çorbası chicken soup with fine noodles

şekerli with sugar

şekerpare small cakes in syrup

şerbet very sweet fruit juice

şıra grape must

şiş kebap small pieces of lamb grilled on skewers

şiş köfte grilled meatballs on skewers

tahin tahini, sesame oil

talaş böreği flaky pastry parcels with meat and vegetable filling

talaş kebabı lamb baked in pastry

tarama roe paté

tarator sauce with walnuts, sesame oil, and garlic

tarhana çorbası traditional soup made with pieces of dried flour, tomato, onion, milk and herbs

tas kebabı goulash-like lamb and vegetable stew

tatlı şarap sweet wine

tava pan (fried)

tavuk budu chicken legs

tavuk döner chicken grilled on spits and carved in thin slices

tavuk dürüm grilled chicken slices rolled in flat bread

tavuk göğsü rice-flour pudding with chicken breast (dessert)

tavuk güveç chicken and vegetable casserole

tavuk kanat grilled chicken wings

tavuklu pilav rice with chicken pieces

tavuk suyu chicken broth

tavuk suyu çorbası soup with chicken broth

tavuk şiş chicken pieces grilled on skewers

taze börülce salatası runner bean salad

taze fasulye green beans in tomato sauce

terbiyeli köfte meatballs with egg and lemon sauce

ton balığı salatası tuna salad

tost toasted sandwich with various fillings

toz şeker granulated sugar

tulumba tatlısı semolina doughnut in syrup

tulum peyniri goat's-milk cheese

turşu pickled vegetables

turşu suyu juice of pickled vegetables

Türk kahvesi Turkish coffee

türlü stewed vegetables and meat

un çorbası flour soup

un helvası halva made of flour, butter and sugar

urfa dürüm grilled meatballs on skewers rolled in flat bread (not spicy)

urfa kebap grilled meatballs on skewers (not spicy)

uskumru dolması stuffed mackerel

üzüm pekmezi grape molasses

üzüm suyu grape juice

vezir parmağı finger-shaped cakes in syrup

vişne sour cherries, morello

vişne suyu sour-cherry juice

yahni meat stewed with onions and vegetables

yaprak sarma (dolma) stuffed vine leaves

yayla çorbası soup made with yoghurt, rice and butter in meat stock

yaz türlüsü stewed summer vegetables

yenibahar allspice

yeşil mercimek çorbası green lentil soup

yeşil salata salad made with lettuce and other fresh greens

yeşil zeytin green olives

yoğurt çorbası soup made with yoghurt

yoğurtlu with yoghurt

yoğurtlu bakla fresh broad beans served with yoghurt

yoğurtlu biber kızartması fried green peppers served with yoghurt

yoğurtlu ıspanak spinach with yoghurt

yoğurtlu kabak kızartması fried courgettes served with yoghurt

yoğurtlu kebap kebab served with yoghurt and pitta bread

yoğurtlu patlıcan kızartması grilled aubergines served with yoghurt

yoğurt tatlısı sponge cake in syrup (dessert)

yumurtalı with egg

zeytinyağlı with olive oil, general name for dishes cooked in olive oil and served cold

zeytinyağlı biber dolması stuffed peppers in olive oil

zeytinyağlı enginar artichokes in olive oil

zeytinyağlı kereviz celeriac cooked in olive oil

zeytinyağlı pırasa leeks in olive oil

zeytinyağlı taze bakla fresh broad beans in olive oil

zeytinyağlı taze fasulye green beans cooked in tomato sauce and olive oil

zeytinyağlı yaprak dolması (sarma) vine leaves stuffed with rice, pine nuts and raisins

Reference

Alphabet

· ·

There are 29 letters in the Turkish alphabet. Here
they are with the letters we use to represent them
in our phonetic transcriptions.

	Sound	**As in**
A a	a	car
B b	b	bed, bad
C c	dj	judge, jam, joint
Ç ç	ch	church, change
D d	d	dodge, did
E e	e	etch, test, red
F f	f	fetch, effort
G g	g	get, garden, go
Ğ ğ		(no sound, makes preceding vowel longer)
H h	h	hedge, how
I ı	uh	speaker, letter
İ i	ee	meet, bin
J j	zh	pleasure, leisure

K k	k	kettle, kitten, cold
L l	l	ledge, lorry
M m	m	mat, man
N n	n	not, no
O o	o	note, only
Ö ö	ur	curt, bird (with rounded lips)
P p	p	pot, pen
R r	r	rot (rolled)
S s	s	sock, sea, sun
Ş ş	sh	shop, sheep, short
T t	t	top, tea
U u	oo	pool, pull, put
Ü ü	ew	Lübeck in German, musée in French, nude and Tewkesbury in English
V v	v	vodka, vision
Y y	y	you, yes
Z z	z	zoo, horizon

Measurements and quantities

1 lb = approx. 0.5 kilo
1 pint = approx. 0.5 litre

Liquids

half a litre of...	**yarım litre...**
	ya-ruhm leet-re...
one litre of...	**bir litre...**
	beer leet-re...
2 litres of...	**iki litre...**
	ee-kee leet-re...
a carafe/jug of...	**bir sürahi...**
	beer sew-ra-hee...
a bottle of...	**bir şişe...**
	beer shee-she...
a glass of...	**bir bardak...**
	beer bar-dak...

Weights

100 grams of...	**yüz gram...**
	yewz gram...
half a kilo of...	**yarım kilo...**
	ya-ruhm kee-lo...
one kilo of...	**bir kilo...**
	beer kee-lo...
2 kilos of...	**iki kilo...**
	ee-kee kee-lo...

Reference

Food

a slice of...	**bir dilim...**
	beer dee-leem...
a portion of...	**bir porsiyon...**
	beer por-see-yon...
a dozen	**bir düzine**
	beer dew-zee-ne
a box/tin of...	**bir kutu...**
	beer koo-too...
a carton of...	**bir karton...**
	beer kar-ton...
a packet of...	**bir paket...**
	beer pa-ket...
a jar of...	**bir kavanoz...**
	beer ka-va-noz...

Numbers

. . . .

In Turkish, numbers are followed by the singular.
So you ask for six peach, two tea, seven stamp etc.

0	**sıfır** suh-fuhr
1	**bir** beer
2	**iki** ee-kee
3	**üç** ewch
4	**dört** durt

5	**beş** besh
6	**altı** al-tuh
7	**yedi** ye-dee
8	**sekiz** se-keez
9	**dokuz** do-kooz
10	**on** on
11	**on bir** on beer
12	**on iki** on ee-kee
13	**on üç** on ewch
14	**on dört** on durt
15	**on beş** on besh
16	**on altı** on al-tuh
17	**on yedi** on ye-dee
18	**on sekiz** on se-keez
19	**on dokuz** on do-kooz
20	**yirmi** yeer-mee
21	**yirmi bir** yeer-mee beer
22	**yirmi iki** yeer-mee ee-kee
30	**otuz** o-tooz
40	**kırk** kuhrk
50	**elli** el-lee
60	**altmış** alt-muhsh
70	**yetmiş** yet-meesh
80	**seksen** sek-sen
90	**doksan** dok-san

100	**yüz** yewz	
200	**iki yüz** ee-kee yewz	
300	**üç yüz** ewch yewz	
400	**dört yüz** durt yewz	
500	**beş yüz** besh yewz	
1000	**bin** been	
2000	**iki bin** ee-kee been	
3000	**üç bin** ewch been	
10,000	**on bin** on been	
100,000	**yüz bin** yewz-been	
1,000,000	**bir milyon** beer meel-yon	

first	**ilk/birinci**	eelk/bee-reen-djee
second	**ikinci**	ee-keen-djee
third	**üçüncü**	ew-chewn-djew
fourth	**dördüncü**	dur-dewn-djew
fifth	**beşinci**	be-sheen-djee
sixth	**altıncı**	al-tuhn-djuh
seventh	**yedinci**	ye-deen-djee
eighth	**sekizinci**	se-kee-zeen-djee
ninth	**dokuzuncu**	do-koo-zoon-djoo
tenth	**onuncu**	o-noon-djoo

Days and months

· ·

Days

Monday	**Pazartesi**	pa-zar-te-see
Tuesday	**Salı**	sa-luh
Wednesday	**Çarşamba**	char-sham-ba
Thursday	**Perşembe**	per-shem-be
Friday	**Cuma**	djoo-ma
Saturday	**Cumartesi**	djoo-mar-te-see
Sunday	**Pazar**	pa-zar

Months

January	**Ocak**	o-djak
February	**Şubat**	shoo-bat
March	**Mart**	mart
April	**Nisan**	nee-san
May	**Mayıs**	ma-yuhs
June	**Haziran**	ha-zee-ran
July	**Temmuz**	tem-mooz
August	**Ağustos**	a-oos-tos
September	**Eylül**	ey-lewl
October	**Ekim**	e-keem
November	**Kasım**	ka-suhm
December	**Aralık**	a-ra-luhk

Reference

Seasons

spring	**ilkbahar**	eelk-ba-har
summer	**yaz**	yaz
autumn	**sonbahar**	son-ba-har
winter	**kış**	kuhsh

Time

. . . .

The 24-hour clock is used on timetables etc.

a.m. (morning)	**sabah**	sa-bah
It's midday	**Öğlen**	ur-len
p.m. (afternoon)	**öğleden sonra**	ur-le-den son-ra
It's...	**Saat…**	sa-at…
It's one o'clock	**Saat bir**	sa-at beer
It's two o'clock	**Saat iki**	sa-at ee-kee
What time is it?	**Saat kaç?**	sa-at kach?

9.00	**dokuz** do-kooz
9.10	**dokuzu on geçiyor/dokuz on** do-koo-zoo on ge-chee-yor/ do-kooz on
9.15	**dokuzu çeyrek geçiyor/dokuz on beş** do-koo-zoo chey-rek ge-chee-yor/ do-kooz on besh
9.30	**dokuz buçuk** do-kooz boo-chook
9.45	**ona çeyrek var/dokuz kırk beş** o-na chey-rek var/do-kooz kuhrk besh
9:50	**ona on var/dokuz elli** o-na on var/do-kooz el-lee
What is the date?	**Bugün ayın kaçı?** boo-gewn a-yuhn ka-chuh?
It's the 16th September 2016	**On altı Eylül ikibin on altı** on al-tuh ey-lewl ee-kee-been on al-tuh
today	**bugün** boo-gewn
tomorrow	**yarın** ya-ruhn
yesterday	**dün** dewn

Time phrases

. . . .

When does it begin/finish?	**Ne zaman başlıyor/bitiyor?** ne za-man bash-luh-yor/ bee-tee-yor?
When does it open/close?	**Ne zaman açılır/kapanır?** ne za-man a-chuh-luhr/ ka-pa-nuhr?
When does it leave?	**Ne zaman kalkıyor?** ne za-man kal-kuh-yor?
When does it return?	**Ne zaman dönüyor?** ne za-man duh-nuh-yor?
at 3 o'clock	**Saat üçte** sa-at ewch-te
before 3 o'clock	**üçten önce** ooch-ten urn-dje
after 3 o'clock	**üçten sonra** ooch-ten son-ra
in the morning	**sabah** sa-bah
this morning	**bu sabah** boo sa-bah
in the afternoon (until dusk)	**öğleden sonra** ur-le-den son-ra
in the evening (after dusk)	**akşam** ak-sham
in an hour's time	**bir saat içinde** sa-at ee-chen-de

142

Public holidays

. . . .

1 January	**Yeni Yıl** New Year's Day
23 April	**Çocuk Bayramı** Children's Day (anniversary of the opening of the first Parliament)
1 May	**Emek ve Dayanışma Bayramı** Labour and Solidarity Day
19 May	**Gençlik ve Spor Bayramı** Youth & Sports Day
30 August	**Zafer Bayramı** Victory Day
29 October	**Cumhuriyet Bayramı** Republic Day

There are two major Islamic religious holidays, both called **Bayram**, each lasting 3-5 days. They are determined by the lunar calendar, so their dates vary from year to year. The first one is the Feast of Ramadan (**Ramazan Bayramı**), which marks the end of the holy month of Ramadan, the second is the Feast of Sacrifice (**Kurban Bayramı**), the most important holiday of the year, when thousands of sheep are slaughtered for the festival.

Phonetic map

• •

When travelling in Turkey, you will need to bear in mind that place names as we know them are not necessarily the same in Turkish. Imagine being at a train station and not recognising the name of your destination when called out! This handy map eliminates such problems by indicating the locations and local pronunciations of major towns and cities.

İstanbul
ee-stan-bool

Bursa
boor-sa

Ankara
an-ka-

İzmir
eez-meer

Antalya
an-tal-ya

Konya
kon-ya

Mersin
mer-seen

Kayseri
kay-se-ree

Samsun
sam-soon

Trabzon
tuh-rab-zon

Kars
kars

Samsun

Trabzon

Kars

Kayseri

Van
van

Malatya

Diyarbakır

Mardin

Gaziantep

Mardin
mar-deen

Malatya
ma-lat-ya

Diyarbakır
dee-yar-ba-kuhr

Gaziantep
ga-zee-an-tep

Grammar

The aim of this section is not to teach you Turkish but just to give you a rough idea of how the language works, and help you understand which parts of the Turkish translations refer to which words in the English. You'll see plenty of exceptions!

Word formation

. . . .

In English you can make new words by adding something to the beginning or end of the first word. You can start with a singular noun and add '-s' for a plural (e.g. 'dog/dogs'), or add '-ed' to a verb to make the past tense, (e.g. 'fill/filled'). Turkish does this all the time, often instead of using separate words like 'my' or 'from'. For example, 'hand' is **el**; 'hands' is **eller**; 'my hands' is **ellerim**; 'in my hands' is **ellerimde**, and so on.

An important feature of Turkish is that there are two types of vowels, and each word (usually) uses vowels of only one type. There are exceptions to this, usually foreign words, in which case the last vowel is the important one.

'back' vowels: **a ı o u**

'front' vowels: **e i ö ü**

This is known as 'vowel harmony', and you need to know about it in order to make up plurals and so on correctly. For example, to say 'from' in Turkish you add -**dan** or -**den** to the word, but the form you use depends on whether the word has back vowels or front vowels. (The hyphen is just to show that they aren't full words in their own right, just endings.)

the beach **plaj**	from the beach **plajdan**
the hotel **otel**	from the hotel **otelden**
London **Londra**	from London **Londra'dan**

Nouns

. . . .

There is no gender in Turkish, i.e. no masculine or feminine nouns as in French (le café, la tête), and this applies to people too, so that 'he' and 'she' are the same.There is also no separate word for 'the' (the definite article) in Turkish. For example, **çay** could mean either 'tea' or 'the tea', according to context. For 'a' (the indefinite article) you use the same word as 'one' **bir kahve** 'a coffee' or 'one coffee'.

a coffee	**bir kahve**
a tea	**bir çay**
an apple	**bir elma**

147

Pronouns

• •

The words for 'I', 'you' etc. are given below. They are only used for extra emphasis, since you know from the verb ending who is being referred to. Remember that you will see them in many different forms according to the grammar of the sentence, e.g. 'they' could appear as **onlar, onları, onlara, onlarda** or **onlardan,** so the best thing is just to watch out for the part at the beginning that stays the same, in other words **ben-, sen-, onlar-,** etc.

Note that 'he', 'she' and 'it' are all the same in Turkish.

There are two words for 'you', since Turkish, like French, makes a distinction between speaking to one person with whom you are on friendly terms, and speaking to several people or someone you do not know well. As a tourist, you are not likely to use the singular 'you' **sen** and will use the more formal **siz** instead.

Verbs

. . . .

Verbs are generally shown with the ending -**mak** or
-**mek**, which is the infinitive (like 'to' in English or
the '-er' ending on a French verb such as 'aller'),
e.g: **koşmak** 'to run', **içmek** 'to drink'. To make a
present tense (e.g. 'I am drinking') you take the
base (e.g. **iç**) and add -**iyor** (continuous tense) plus
the relevant 'person' ending to show who is doing
the action, in this case -**um** for 'I':

içmek – içiyorum

Because of these different endings for different
people, there's usually no need in Turkish for a
separate pronoun like 'I', 'you', etc.

We don't have space to go into the different cases
and tenses here, but we have given you as many
phrases as possible in the dictionary, as well as in
the alphabetical topics themselves. Just remember,
the form in which a verb appears in a dictionary
may be very different from the one it takes when
used in context. The part to look for is the 'base' or
'root' (e.g. **iç**- in the example above) which tells you
what the action is (e.g. 'drinking'); you can probably
tell from the ending who is doing the action.

Negatives

. . . .

Negatives in Turkish are formed using -mı/-mu/
-mi/-mü, which comes immediately after the root,
e.g. **iste-** or **git-** (which sometimes appears as **gid**):

I want	**istiyorum**
I don't want	**istemiyorum**
He does not want	**istemiyor**
I am going	**gidiyorum**
I am not going	**gitmiyorum**
You are not going	**gitmiyorsun**
They are not going	**gitmiyorlar**

Questions

. . . .

Questions are formed using the same element
-mı/-mu/-mi/-mü, but in a different position: instead
of coming immediately after the root, it (usually)
comes immediately before the part of the word
corresponding to the pronoun, e.g. **-sunuz** 'you':

Do you want...?	**...istiyor musunuz?**
Does he want...?	**...istiyor mu?**
Are you going?	**gidiyor musunuz?**
Are they going?	**gidiyorlar mı?**

Grammar

Adjectives

Adjectives come before nouns and the verb comes at the end, e.g. 'the woman a dog saw' not 'the woman saw a dog'.

There are no special forms of adjectives (comparatives) to express 'more', like English 'good/better/best'. You just say 'more good', 'most good' etc. **Daha** is the word for 'more' and **en** is the word for 'most':

a new house	**yeni bir ev**
a pretty girl	**güzel bir kız**
a newer house	**daha yeni bir ev**
a prettier girl	**daha güzel bir kız**
the newest house	**en yeni ev**
the prettiest girl	**en güzel kız**

List of useful endings

Here are some more of the most important endings. With names of people, places etc. (proper nouns), there is an apostrophe before the ending, e.g. **İstanbul'a** not **İstanbula**. Incidentally, 'for' is not expressed by an ending but by a separate word (**için**).

TO: -ya/-a (back vowel), **-ye/-e** (front vowel)

plaja = to the beach
eve = to the house (home)
İstanbul'a = to Istanbul
İngiltere'ye = to England

FROM: -dan/-tan (back), **-den/-ten** (front)

plajdan = from the beach
evden = from home
İstanbul'dan = from Istanbul
İngiltere'den = from England

IN, ON, AT: -da/-ta (back), **-de/-te** (front)

plajda = on the beach
evde = at home
Londra'da = in London
İngiltere'de = in England

BY, WITH: -la/-yla (back), **-le/-yle** (front)

uçakla = by plane
otobüsle = by bus
arabayla = by car
Hasan'la = with Hasan
Ali'yle = with Ali

WITHOUT: -sız/-suz (back), **-siz/-süz** (front)

parasız = without money
sütsüz = without milk
buzsuz = without ice
şekersiz = without sugar

English – Turkish
Turkish – English

A

a(n)	bir	beer
about	hakkında	hak-kuhn-da
above	üstünde	ews-tewn-de
to accept	kabul etmek	ka-bool et-mek
do you accept Visa®?	Visa® kartı alıyor musunuz?	visa kar-tuh a-luh-yor-moo-soo-nooz?
accident	kaza	ka-za
ache: *it aches*	ağrıyor	a-ruh-yor
address	adres	ad-res
admission charge	giriş ücreti	gee-reesh ewdj-re-tee
adult	yetişkin	ye-teesh-keen
aeroplane	uçak	oo-chak
after	sonra	son-ra
afternoon	öğleden sonra	ur-le-den son-ra
this afternoon	bu öğleden sonra	boo ur-le-den son-ra
in the afternoon	öğleden sonra	ur-le-den son-ra
tomorrow afternoon	yarın öğleden sonra	ya-ruhn ur-le-den son-ra
again	tekrar	tek-rar
age	yaş	yash
agent	acenta	a-djen-ta
estate agent	emlakçı	em-lak-chuh
travel agent	seyahat acentası	se-ya-hat a-djen-ta-suh
ago	önce	urn-dje
ahead: *straight ahead*	düz ileri	dewz ee-le-ree
air conditioning	klima	kuh-lee-ma
airport	havaalanı; havalimanı	ha-va-a-la-nuh; ha-va-lee-ma-nuh
alarm	alarm	a-larm
alarm clock	çalar saat	cha-lar sa-at
alcohol	alkol	al-kol
without alcohol	alkolsüz	al-kol-sewz
all	hepsi	hep-see

154

to be allergic to	alerjisi var	a-ler-zhee-see var
all right (ok)	tamam; peki	ta-mam; pe-kee
are you all right?	iyi misiniz?	ee-yee mee-see-nez?
I'm all right	iyiyim	ee-yee-yeem
alone	yalnız	yal-nuhz
always	her zaman	her za-man
ambulance	ambülans	am-bew-lans
America	Amerika	a-me-ree-ka
American	Amerikalı	a-me-ree-ka-luh
and	ve	ve
angry	kızgın	kuhz-guhn
I'm angry	kızgınım	kuhz-guh-nuhm
another	bir … daha	beer … da-ha
another beer	bir bira daha	beer bee-ra da-ha
answer	cevap	dje-vap
there's no answer (phone)	cevap vermiyor	dje-vap ver-mee-yor
to answer	cevap vermek	dje-vap ver-mek
answering machine	telesekreter	te-le sek-re-ter
ants	karıncalar	ka-ruhn-dja-lar
any: *have you any matches?*	kibritiniz var mı?	keeb-ree-tee-neez var-muh?
apartment	daire	da-ee-re
apple	elma	el-ma
apple juice	elma suyu	el-ma soo-yoo
April	Nisan	nee-san
arm	kol	kol
my arm hurts	kolum ağrıyor	ko-loom a-ruh-yor
to arrest	tutuklamak	too-took-la-mak
arrivals	geliş; varış	ge-leesh; va-ruhsh
to arrive	varmak	var-mak
art gallery	sanat galerisi	sa-nat ga-le-ree-see
artist	sanatçı	sa-nat-chuh
ashtray	kül tablası	kewl tab-la-suh
asthma	astım	as-tuhm

at	-de/da	see GRAMMAR
to attack	saldırmak	sal-duhr-mak
I've been attacked	saldırıya uğradım	sal-duh-ruh-ya oo-ra-duhm
attack	saldırı	sal-duh-ruh
heart attack	kalp krizi	kalp kree-zee
attention	dikkat	deek-kat
attractive	çekici	che-kee-djee
August	Ağustos	aa-oos-tos
aunt (maternal)	teyze	tey-ze
(paternal)	hala	ha-la
Australia	Avusturalya	a-voos-too-ral-ya
Australian	Avusturalyalı	a-voos-too-ral-ya-luh
automatic car	otomatik araba	o-to-ma-teek a-ra-ba
autumn	sonbahar	son-ba-har
away: *please go away!*	lütfen gidin!	lewt-fen gee-deen!

B

baby	bebek	be-bek
baby food	bebek maması	be-bek ma-ma-suh
baby-sitter	bebek bakıcısı	be-bek ba-kuh-djuh-suh
back (of body)	sırt	suhrt
backpack	sırt çantası	suhrt chan-ta-suh
bad	kötü	kur-tew
bag	çanta	chan-ta
baggage	bagaj	ba-gazh
baggage reclaim	bagaj alma yeri	ba-gazh al-ma-ye-ree
baker's	fırın	fuh-rurn
ball	top	top
bandage	bandaj	ban-dazh
bank	banka	ban-ka
where is the bank?	banka nerede?	ban-ka ne-re-de?
bar	bar	bar

barber	berber	ber-ber
bargain	pazarlık	pa-zar-luhk
no bargaining	pazarlık yapılmaz	pa-zar-luhk ya-puhl-maz
basket	sepet	se-pet
bath	banyo	ban-yo
(Turkish bath)	hamam	ha-mam
bathroom	banyo	ban-yo
where is the bathroom?	tuvalet nerede?	tu-va-let ne-re-de?
with bathroom	banyolu	ban-yo-loo
battery (for car)	akü	a-kew
(for torch, camera)	pil	peel
the battery is flat	pil bitti	peel beet-tee
I need batteries for this	bunun için pil istiyorum	boo-noon ee-cheen peel ees-tee-yo-room
bazaar	pazar	pa-zar
where is the bazaar?	pazar nerede?	pa-zar ne-re-de?
be	olmak	ol-mak
beach	plaj	puh-lazh
how far is the beach?	plaj ne kadar uzaklıkta?	puh-lazh ne ka-dar oo-zak-luhk-ta?
beautiful	güzel	gew-zel
bed	yatak	ya-tak
double bed	çift kişilik yatak	cheeft kee-shee-leek ya-tak
twin beds	iki tek yatak	ee-kee tek ya-tak
bedclothes	yatak takımları	ya-tak ta-kuhm-la-ruh
I need more bedclothes	başka daha yatak takımı var mı	bash-ka da-ha ya-tak ta-kuh-muh var muh
these bedclothes are dirty	bu yatak takımları kirli	boo ya-tak ta-kuhm-la-ruh keer-lee
bedroom	yatak odası	ya-tak o-da-suh
double bedroom	çift kişilik yatak odası	cheeft kee-shee-leek ya-tak o-da-suh

157

single bedroom	tek kişilik yatak odası	tek kee-shee-leek ya-tak o-da-suh
bee	arı	a-ruh
beef	sığır eti	suh-uhr e-tee
beer	bira	bee-ra
a glass of beer	bir bardak bira	beer bar-dak bee-ra
a bottle of beer	bir şişe bira	beer shee-she bee-ra
before	önce	urn-dje
before 4 o'clock	saat 4'den önce	sa-at durt-ten urn-dje
before dinner	yemekten önce	ye-mek-ten urn-dje
to begin	başlamak	bash-la-mak
behind	arkada; geride	ar-ka-da; ge-ree-de
to believe	inanmak	ee-nan-mak
I don't believe you	sana inanmıyorum	sa-na ee-nan-muh-yo-room
belly dancing	göbek dansı	gur-bek dan-suh
below	altında	al-tuhn-da
belt	kemer	ke-mer
money belt	para kemeri	pa-ra ke-me-ree
seat belt	emniyet kemeri	em-nee-yet ke-me-ree
bend	viraj	vee-razh
beside (next to)	yanında	ya-nuhn-da
best	en iyi	en ee-yee
better (than)	daha iyi	da-ha ee-yee
bicycle	bisiklet	bee-seek-let
big	büyük	bew-yewk
bigger	daha büyük	da-ha bew-yewk
biggest	en büyük	en bew-yewk
bill	hesap	he-sap
the bill, please	hesap, lütfen	he-sap, lewt-fen
there's a mistake on the bill	hesapta yanlışlık var	he-sap-ta yan-luhsh-luhk var
bin (for rubbish)	çöp kutusu	churp koo-too-soo
bird	kuş	koosh
birthday	doğum günü	do-oom gew-new

happy birthday!	doğum gününü kutlu olsun!	do-oom gew-newn koot-loo ol-soon!
birthday card	doğum günü kartı	do-oom gew-new kar-tuh
biscuits	bisküvi	bees-kew-vee
bit: *a bit*	bir parça	beer par-cha
bite (insect, dog)	ısırık	uh-suh-ruhk
I've been bitten by a dog	beni bir köpek ısırdı	be-nee beer kur-pek uh-suhr-duh
I've been bitten by a snake	beni bir yılan soktu	be-nee beer yuh-lan sok-too
bitter (taste)	acı	a-djuh
black	siyah	see-yah
blanket	battaniye	bat-ta-nee-ye
to bleed	kanamak	ka-na-mak
blind (person)	kör	kur
blinds (on window)	panjur	pan-zhoor
blister	su toplaması	soo top-la-ma-suh
blocked	tıkandı	tuh-kan-duh
the sink is blocked	lavabo tıkandı	la-va-bo tuh-kan-duh
blood	kan	kan
blood group	kan grubu	kan goo-roo-boo
blood pressure	tansiyon	tan-see-yon
blue	mavi	ma-vee
boarding card	uçuş kartı	oo-choosh kar-tuh
boat	vapur; tekne	va-poor; tek-ne
boat trip	tekne turu	tek-ne too-roo
is there a boat trip?	tekne turu var mı?	tek-ne too-roo var-muh?
when is the boat trip?	tekne turu ne zaman?	tek-ne too-roo ne za-man?
boiled (food)	kaynamış	kay-na-mush
I need boiled water	kaynamış su istiyorum	kay-na-mush soo ees-tee-yo-room
bone	kemik	ke-meek
book	kitap	kee-tap

to book	yer ayırtmak	yer a-yuhrt-mak
I've booked	ayırttım	a-yuhrt-tuhm
booking	rezervasyon	re-zer-vas-yon
bookshop	kitapçı	kee-tap-chuh
boots	çizme	cheez-me
boring: it's boring	sıkıcı	suh-kuh-djuh
both: I'd like both	her ikisini de	her ee-kee-see-nee de
bottle	şişe	shee-she
a bottle of water	bir şişe su	beer shee-she soo
a bottle of wine	bir şişe şarap	beer shee-she sha-rap
bottle-opener	bir şişe açacağı	beer shee-she a-cha-dja-uh
box	kutu	koo-too
box office	gişe	gee-she
boy	erkek çocuk	er-kek cho-djook
boyfriend	erkek arkadaş	er-kek ar-ka-dash
brandy	brendi; konyak	bren-dee; kon-yak
bread	ekmek	ek-mek
do you sell bread?	ekmek var mı?	ek-mek var muh?
some bread, please	biraz ekmek, lütfen	bee-raz ek-mek, lewt-fen
to break	kırmak	kuhr-mak
to break down (car)	bozulmak	bo-zool-mak
breakfast	kahvaltı	kah-val-tuh
what is there for breakfast?	kahvaltıda ne var?	kah-val-tuh-da ne var?
what time is breakfast?	kahvaltı ne zaman?	kah-val-tuh ne za-man?
breakfast included	kahvaltı dahil	kah-val-tuh da-heel
to breathe	nefes almak	ne-fes al-mak
bring	getirmek	ge-teer-mek
what should I bring?	ne getireyim?	ne ge-tee-re-yeem?
British	İngiliz	een-gee-leez
I'm British	İngilizim	een-gee-lee-zeem

brochure	broşür	bro-shewr
have you a brochure in English?	İngilizce broşürünüz var mı?	een-gee-leez-dje bro-shew-rew-newz var muh?
broken	kırık	kuh-ruhk
broken down (car, machine)	bozuldu	bo-zool-doo
brother	erkek kardeş	er-kek kar-desh
brown	kahverengi	kah-ve-ren-gee
brush	fırça	fuhr-cha
hairbrush	saç fırçası	sach fuhr-cha-suh
toothbrush	diş fırçası	deesh fuhr-cha-suh
bucket	kova	ko-va
bulb (light)	ampul	am-pool
bureau de change	döviz bürosu	dur-veez bew-ro-soo
burglary: there's been a buglary	bir soygun oldu	beer soy-goon ol-doo
burn	yanık	ya-nuhk
to burn	yanmak	yan-mak
I've burned my hand	elim yandı	e-leem yan-duh
burnt: it's burnt	yanmış; yanık	yan-muhsh; ya-nuhk
bus	otobüs	o-to-bews
can I go by bus?	otobüsle gidebilir miyim?	o-to-bews-le gee-de-bee-leer mee-yeem?
the bus to the beach	plaja giden otobüs	pla-zha gee-den o-to-bews
the bus to the centre	şehre giden otobüs	sheh-re gee-den o-to-bews
business	iş	eesh
bus station	otobüs terminali; otogar	o-to-bews ter-mee-na-lee; o-to-gar
where is the bus station?	otogar nerede?	o-to-gar ne-re-de?
bus stop	otobüs durağı	o-to-bews doo-ra-uh
where is the bus stop?	otobüs durağı nerede?	o-to-bews doo-ra-uh ne-re-de?

161

busy: *I'm busy*	meşgulüm	mesh-goo-lewm
butcher's	kasap	ka-sap
butter	tereyağı	te-re-ya-uh
to buy	satın almak	sa-tuhn al-mak
where can I buy milk?	nereden süt alabilirim?	ne-re-den sewt a-la-bee-lee-reem?
where can I buy bread?	nereden ekmek alabilirim?	ne-re-den ek-mek a-la-bee-lee-reem?
can I buy this?	bunu alabilir miyim?	boo-noo a-la-bee-leer mee-yeem?
by	ile	ee-le
by bus	otobüs ile (otobüsle)	o-to-bews-le
by train	tren ile (trenle)	tren-le

C

café	kafe	ka-fe
cake	kek	kek
cake shop	pastane	pas-ta-ne
to call (on phone)	telefon etmek	te-le-fon et-mek
camcorder	video kamera	vi-de-o ka-me-ra
camel	deve	de-ve
camera	fotoğraf makinası	fo-to-raf ma-kee-na-suh
to camp	kamp yapmak	kamp yap-mak
no camping	kamp yapmak yasaktır	kamp yap-mak ya-sak-tuhr
campsite	kamp yeri; kamping	kamp-ye-ree; kam-peeng
where is the campsite?	kamp yeri nerede?	kamp ye-ree ne-re-de?
can (of food)	teneke kutu; konserve kutusu	te-ne-ke koo-too; kon-ser-ve koo-too-soo
a can of oil	bir teneke yağ	beer te-ne-ke ya
cancel	iptal etmek	eep-tal et-mek

I want to cancel my booking	rezervasyonumu iptal etmek istiyorum	re-zer-vas-yo-noo-moo eep-tal et-mek ees-tee-yo-room
candle	mum	moom
can-opener	konserve açacağı	kon-ser-ve a-cha-dja-uh
car	araba	a-ra-ba
by car	arabayla	a-ra-bay-la
caravan	karavan	ka-ra-van
card	kart	kart
cards (playing)	oyun kağıdı	o-yoon ka-uh-duh
car park	otopark	oto-park
carpet (rug)	halı	ha-luh
carry	taşımak	ta-shuh-mak
car seat (for child)	çocuk koltuğu	cho-djook kol-too-oo
car wash	araba yıkama	a-ra-ba yuh-ka-ma
cash	nakit	na-keet
I have no cash	nakit param yok	na-keet pa-ram yok
to cash	bozdurmak	boz-door-mak
cash desk	kasa; vezne	ka-sa; vez-ne
castle	kale	ka-le
cat	kedi	ke-dee
caution	dikkat	deek-kat
cave	mağara	ma-a-ra
CD	CD	see-dee
do you have it on CD?	CD's var mi?	see-dee-see var-muh?
CD player	CD çalar	see-dee cha-lar
cemetery	mezarlık	me-zar-luhk
central	merkezi	mer-ke-zee
central station	merkez istasyon	mer-kez ees-tas-yon
centre	merkezi	mer-ke-zee
town centre	şehir merkezi	she-heer mer-ke-zee
certificate	sertifika	ser-tee-fee-ka
chain	zincir	zeen-djeer
chair	sandalye	san-dal-ye

champagne	şampanya	sham-pan-ya
change (coins)	bozuk para	bo-zook pa-ra
where's my change?	paramın üstü nerede?	pa-ra-muhn ews-tew ne-re-de?
keep the change	üstü kalsın	ews-tew kal-suhn
to change (money)	bozdurmak	boz-door-mak
where can I change money?	nerede para bozdurabilirim?	ne-re-de pa-ra boz-doo-ra-bee-lee-reem?
changing-room	soyunma kabini	so-yoon-ma ka-bee-nee
charge (fee)	ücret	ewdj-ret
cheap	ucuz	oo-djooz
I want the cheapest	en ucuzunu istiyorum	en oo-djoo-zoo-noo ees-tee-yo-room
check	kontrol	kon-trol
to check in	check in; yapmak; giriş yapmak	chek-in; yap-mak; gee-reesh yap-mak
what time should I check in?	ne zaman check in yapmalıyım?; ne zaman giriş yapmalıyım?	ne za-man chek een yap-ma-luh-yuhm?; ne za-man gee-reesh yap-ma-luh-yuhm?
cheers!	şerefe!	she-re-fe!
cheese	peynir	pey-neer
chemist's	eczane	edj-za-ne
where is the chemist's?	eczane nerede?	edj-za-ne ne-re-de?
night duty chemist	nöbetçi eczane	nur-bet-chee edj-za-ne
cheque	çek	chek
cheque book	çek defteri	chek def-te-ree
travellers' cheques	seyahat çeki	se-ya-hat chek-ee
cherry	kiraz	kee-raz
chest (of body)	göğüs	gur-ews
chewing-gum	çiklet	cheek-let
chickenpox	suçiçeği	soo-chee-che-ee
child	çocuk	cho-djook
chips	patates tava	pa-ta-tes ta-va

chocolate	çikolata	chee-ko-la-ta
hot chocolate	kakao	ka-ka-o
chop (meat)	pirzola	peer-zo-la
Christmas	Noel	no-el
church	kilise	kee-lee-se
cigar	puro	poo-ro
cigarettes	sigara	see-ga-ra
a packet of cigarettes	bir paket sigara	beer pa-ket see-ga-ra
cinema	sinema	see-ne-ma
where is the cinema?	sinema nerede?	see-ne-ma ne-re-de?
what's on at the cinema?	sinemada ne oynuyor?	see-ne-ma-da ne oy-noo-yor?
circus	sirk	seerk
city	şehir	she-heer
city centre	şehir merkezi	she-heer mer-ke-zee
clean	temiz	te-meez
it's not clean	temiz değil	te-meez de-eel
to clean	temizlemek	te-mez-le-mek
please clean the bath	lütfen banyoyu temizleyin	lewt-fen ban-yo-yoo te-meez-le-yeen
please clean my room	lütfen odamı temizleyin	lewt-fen o-da-muh te-meez-le-yeen
climbing: *to go climbing*	dağa tırmanmak	da-a tuhr-man-mak
cloakroom	vestiyer	ves-tee-yer
clock	saat	sa-at
close: *is it close by?*	yakın mı?	ya-kun-muh?
to close	kapatmak	ka-pat-mak
when does it close?	ne zaman kapanır?	ne za-man kap-a-nuhr?
closed	kapalı	ka-pa-luh
is it closed?	kapalı mı?	ka-pa-luh muh?
clothes	giysi	geey-see

165

coast	sahil	sa-heel
coat	palto	pal-to
cocoa	kakao	ka-ka-o
cockroach	hamamböceği	ha-mam-bur-dje-ee
coconut	hindistan cevizi	heen-dees-tan dje-vee-zee
coffee	kahve	kah-ve
black coffee	sütsüz kahve	sewt-sewz kah-ve
iced coffee	buzlu kahve	booz-loo kah-ve
instant coffee	Nescafé®	nes-ka-fe
white coffee	sütlü kahve	sewt-lew kah-ve
coin	bozuk para	bo-zook pa-ra
Coke®	Kola	ko-la
cold: I have a cold	üşüttüm	ew-shewt-tewm
cold	soğuk	so-ook
I'm cold	üşüyorum	ew-shew-yo-room
I'd like a cold drink	soğuk bir içecek lütfen	so-ook beer ee-che-djek lewt-fen
colour	renk	renk
comb	tarak	ta-rak
to come (arrive)	gelmek	gel-mek
come in!	girin!	gee-reen!
comfortable	rahat	ra-hat
company (business)	şirket	sheer-ket
compass	pusula	poo-soo-la
complaint	şikayet	shee-ka-yet
computer	bilgisayar	beel-gee-sa-yar
concert	konser	kon-ser
classical concert	klasik müzik konseri	kuh-la-seek mew-zeek kon-se-ree
pop concert	pop konseri	pop kon-se-ree
conditioner (for hair)	saç kremi	sach kre-mee
condoms	prezervatif	pre-zer-va-teef
conference	konferans	kon-fe-rans
to confirm	teyid etmek	te-yeet et-mek

congratulations!	tebrikler!	teb-reek-ler!
connection (train, plane)	bağlantı	ba-lan-tuh
I missed my connection	aktarmayı kaçırdım	ak-tar-ma-yuh ka-chur-dum
consulate	konsolosluk	kon-so-los-look
British consulate	İngiltere konsolosluğu	een-geel-te-re kon-so-los-loo-oo
American consulate	Amerika konsolosluğu	a-me-ree-ka kon-so-los-loo-oo
contact lens	kontak lens	kon-tak lens
I've lost my contact lenses	kontak lensimi kaybettim	kon-tak len-see-mee kay-bet-teem
contact lens cleaner	kontak lens temizleyici	kon-tak lens te-meez-le-yee-djee-see
contraceptives (pill)	doğum kontrol hapı	do-oom kon-trol ha-puh
to cook	pişirmek	pee-sheer-mek
cooker	ocak	o-djak
copy	kopya	kop-ya
to copy (photocopy)	fotokopi çekmek	fo-to-ko-pee chek-mek
corkscrew	tirbuşon	teer-boo-shon
corner	köşe	kur-she
cost: *how much does it cost?*	ne kadar?	ne ka-dar?
cot	bebek yatağı	be-bek ya-ta-uh
cotton (material)	pamuklu	pa-mook-loo
is it cotton?	pamuklu mu?	pa-mook-loo moo?
to cough	öksürmek	urk-sewr-mek
counter	gişe	gee-she
country (not town)	ülke	ewl-ke
couple (two people)	çift	cheeft
crash (collision)	çarpışma	char-puhsh-ma
crash helmet	kask	kask
cream (dairy)	krema	kuh-re-ma
(cosmetic)	krem	kuh-rem

credit card	kredi kartı	kre-dee kar-tuh
I've lost my credit card	kredi kartımı kaybettim	kre-dee kar-tuh-muh kay-bet-teem
crisps	cips	djeeps
crossroads	kavşak	kav-shak
to cry (weep)	ağlamak	a-la-mak
cucumber	salatalık	sa-la-ta-luhk
cul-de-sac	çıkmaz sokak	chuhk-maz so-kak
cup	fincan	feen-djan
cupboard	dolap	do-lap
currant	kuşüzümü	koosh-ew-zew-mew
current	akıntı	a-kuhn-tuh
cushion	yastık	yas-tuhk
customs	gümrük	gewm-rewk
customs control	gümrük kontrolü	gewm-rewk kon-tro-lew
cut	kesik	ke-seek
to cut	kesmek	kes-mek
to cycle	bisiklete binmek	bee-seek-le-te been-mek

D

daily	günlük	gewn-lewk
damage	zarar	za-rar
dance	dans	dans
to dance	dans etmek	dans et-mek
danger	tehlike	teh-lee-ke
dangerous	tehlikeli	teh-lee-ke-lee
dark	koyu	ko-yoo
date (calendar)	tarih	ta-reeh
what is the date?	bugün tarih nedir?	boo-gewn ta-reeh ne-deer?
date of birth	doğum tarihi	do-oom ta-ree-hee
dates (fruit)	hurma	hoor-ma
daughter	kız çocuk	kuhz cho-djook

dawn	şafak	sha-fak
day	gün	gewn
every day	her gün	her gewn
deaf	sağır	sa-uhr
decaffeinated coffee	kafeinsiz kahve	ka-fe-een-seez kah-ve
December	Aralık	a-ra-luhk
deck chair	şezlong	shez-long
deep	derin	de-reen
delay	gecikme	ge-djeek-me
is there a delay?	gecikme mi var?	ge-djeek-me mee var?
delicatessen	şarküteri	shar-kew-te-ree
delicious: *this is delicious!*	çok lezzetli!	chok lez-zet-lee!
dentist	diş hekimi	deesh he-kee-mee
dentures	protez	pro-tez
deodorant	deodorant	deo-do-rant
department store	büyük mağaza	bew-yewk ma-za
departures	gidiş; ayrılış	gee-deesh;ay-ru-lush
deposit	depozit	de-po-zeet
dessert	tatlı	tat-luh
detergent	deterjan	de-ter-zhan
diabetic	şeker hastası	she-ker has-ta-suh
dialling code	telefon kodu	te-le-fon ko-doo
diamond	elmas	el-mas
diarrhoea	ishal	ees-hal
diary	günlük	gewn-lewk
dictionary	sözlük	surz-lewk
diesel	dizel	dee-zel
where can I get diesel?	nereden dizel benzin alabilirim?	ne-re-den dee-zel ben-zeen a-la-bee-lee-reem?
diet	diyet; perhiz	dee-yet; per-heez
I'm on a diet	diyetteyim; perhizdeyim	dee-yet-te-yeem; per-heez-de-yeem
different	farklı	fark-luh

difficult: *it's difficult*	zor	zor
dinghy	küçük sandal	kew-chewk san-dal
dining room	yemek odası	ye-mek o-da-suh
dinner (evening meal)	akşam yemeği	ak-sham ye-me-ee
direct: *is it a direct train?*	direk tren mi?	dee-rekt tren mee?
direct flight	direk uçuş	dee-rekt oo-choosh
directory (telephone)	telefon rehberi	te-le-fon reh-be-ree
dirty	kirli	keer-lee
disabled (person)	engelli	en-gel-lee
disco	disko	dees-ko
discount	indirim	een-dee-reem
disease	hastalık	has-ta-luhk
disinfectant	dezenfektan	de-zen-fek-tan
distilled water	damıtılmış su	da-muh-tuhl-mush soo
to dive	dalmak	dal-mak
divorced	boşanmış	bo-shan-muhsh
I'm divorced	boşandım	bo-shan-duhm
dizzy: *I feel dizzy*	başım dönüyor	ba-shuhm dur-new-yor
doctor	doktor	dok-tor
documents	dokümanlar	do-kew-man-lar
where are the documents?	dokümanlar/evraklar nerede?	do-kew-man-lar/ev-rak-lar ne-re-de?
dog	köpek	kur-pek
doll	oyuncak bebek	o-yoon-djak be-bek
donkey	eşek	e-shek
door	kapı	ka-puh
double bed	çift kişilik yatak	cheeft kee-shee-leek ya-tak
double room	çift kişilik oda	cheeft kee-shee-leek o-da

downstairs	alt kat	alt kat
dozen	düzine	dew-zee-ne
drain	lâğım	la-uhm
drawer	çekmece	chek-me-dje
dress	elbise	el-bee-se
drink	içecek	ee-che-djeck
to drink	içmek	eech-mek
drinking water	içme suyu	eech-me soo-yoo
to drive	araba sürmek	a-ra-ba sewr-mek
driver	şoför	sho-fur
driving licence	ehliyet	eh-lee-yet
to drown	boğulmak	bo-ool-mak
drug	ilaç	ee-lach
drunk	sarhoş	sar-hosh
I'm drunk	sarhoşum	sar-ho-shoom
dry	kuru	koo-roo
dry-cleaner's	kuru temizleyici	koo-roo te-meez-le-yee-djee
dummy (for baby)	emzik	em-zeek
dust	toz	toz
duty-free	gümrüksüz	gewm-rewk-sewz

E

ear	kulak	koo-lak
ear ache: *I have ear ache*	kulağım ağrıyor	koo-la-uhm a-ruh-yor
early	erken	er-ken
earrings	küpe	kew-pe
earthquake	deprem	dep-rem
east	doğu	do-oo
Easter	Paskalya	pas-kal-ya
easy	kolay	ko-lay
to eat	yemek yemek	ye-mek ye-mek
egg	yumurta	yoo-moor-ta
elastic band	lastik	las-teek

electric	elektrik	e-lek-treek
electric razor	elektrikli traş makinası	e-lek-treek-lee tuh-rash ma-kee-na-suh
e-mail	e-mail	ee-meyl
embassy	büyükelçilik	bew-yewk-el-chee-leek
British embassy	İngiltere büyükelçiliği	een-geel-te-re bew-yewk-el-chee-lee-ee
American embassy	Amerika büyükelçiliği	a-me-ree-ka- bew-yewk-el-chee-lee-ee
emergency	acil durum	a-djeel doo-room
empty	boş	bosh
end	bitmek; son bulmak	beet-mek; son bool-mak
when does it end?	ne zaman biter?	ne za-man bee-ter?
engaged (to be married)	nişanlı	nee-shan-luh
it's engaged (phone, toilet)	meşgul	mesh-gool
engine	motor	mo-tor
England	İngiltere	een-geel-te-re
English (nationality)	İngiliz	een-gee-leez
(language)	İngilizce	een-gee-leez-dje
I'm English	İngilizim	een-gee-lee-zeem
do you speak English?	İngilizce biliyor musunuz?	een-gee-leez-dje bee-lee-yor-moo-soo-nooz?
enjoy: *I enjoy swimming*	yüzmeyi severim	yewz-me-yee se-ve-reem
I enjoy playing tennis	tenis oynamayı severim	te-nees oy-na-ma-yuh se-ve-reem
enough	yeterli	ye-ter-lee
it's not enough	yeterli değil	ye-ter-lee de-eel
enquiry desk	danışma	da-nuhsh-ma
to enter	girmek	geer-mek
entertainment	eğlence	ey-len-dje
entrance	giriş	gee-reesh

where is the entrance?	giriş nerede?	gee-reesh ne-re-de?
entrance fee	giriş ücreti	gee-reesh ewdj-re-tee
envelope	zarf	zarf
escape: fire escape	yangın çıkışı	yan-guhn chuh-kuh-shuh
Europe	Avrupa	av-roo-pa
evening	akşam	ak-sham
this evening	bu akşam	boo ak-sham
tomorrow evening	yarın akşam	ya-ruhn ak-sham
evening meal	akşam yemeği	ak-sham ye-me-ee
every	her	her
every day	her gün	her gewn
every year	her yıl	her yuhl
everyone	herkes	her-kes
excellent	mükemmel	mew-kem-mel
excess luggage	fazla bagaj	faz-la ba-gazh
exchange	kambiyo	kam-bee-yo
exchange rate	döviz kuru	dur-veez koo-roo
exciting	heyecan verici	he-ye-djan ve-ree-djee
excuse me!	afedersiniz!	a-fe-der-see-neez!
exhibition	sergi	ser-gee
exit	çıkış	chuh-kuhsh
where is the exit?	çıkış neresi?	chuh-kuhsh ne-re-de?
emergency exit	acil çıkış	a-djeel chuh-kuhsh
expensive	pahalı	pa-ha-luh
to expire	günü geçmek	gew-new gech-mek
to explain	anlatmak; açıklamak	an-lat-mak; a-chuk-la-mak
please explain	lütfen açıklayın	lewt-fen a-chuhk-la-yuhn
extra	fazla	faz-la
eye	göz	gurz

173

F

face	yüz	yewz
factory	fabrika	fab-ree-ka
to faint	bayılmak	ba-yuhl-mak
to fall	düşmek	dewsh-mek
family	aile	a-ee-le
my family	ailem	a-ee-lem
famous	ünlü	ewn-lew
fan	vantilatör	van-tee-la-tur
far: *is it far?*	uzak mı?	oo-zak muh?
fare (train, bus, etc.)	ücret	ewdj-ret
how much is the fare?	ücreti ne kadar?	ewdj-re-tee ne ka-dar?
farm	çiftlik	cheeft-leek
farmer	çiftçi	cheeft-chee
fashion	moda	mo-da
fast	hızlı	huhz-luh
fat (person)	şişman	sheesh-man
(food)	yağ	ya
fatty	yağlı	ya-luh
father	baba	ba-ba
my father	babam	ba-bam
father-in-law	kayınpeder	ka-yuhn-pe-der
my father-in-law	kayınpederim	ka-yuhn-pe-de-reem
fault (defect)	kusur/hata	koo-soor/ha-ta
favourite	favori	fa-vo-ree
February	Şubat	shoo-bat
feel: *I feel sick*	midem bulanıyor	mee-dem boo-la-nuh-yor
I don't feel well	kendimi iyi hissetmiyorum	ken-dee-mee ee-yee hees-set-mee-yo-room
I feel tired	kendimi yorgun hissediyorum	ken-dee-mee yor-goon hees-se-dee-yo-room
ferry	vapur	va-poor

174

(car ferry)	feribot	fe-ree-bot
few	birkaç	beer-kach
fiancé(e)	nişanlı	nee-shan-luh
to fill (up)	doldurmak	dol-door-mak
fill it up!	doldurun!	dol-doo-roon!
film	film	fee-leem
filter	filtre	feelt-re
to find	bulmak	bool-mak
I can't find my passport	pasaportumu bulamıyorum	pa-sa-por-too-moo boo-la-muh-yo-room
I can't find my wallet	cüzdanımı bulamıyorum	djewz-da-nuh-muh boo-la-muh-yo-room
fine (to be paid)	ceza	dje-za
fine (weather)	güzel	gew-zel
finish: *when does it finish?*	ne zaman biter?	ne za-man bee-ter?
fire	yangın	yan-gun
fire alarm	yangın alarmı	yan-guhn a-lar-muh
fire brigade	itfaiye	eet-fa-ee-ye
fire exit	yangın çıkışı	yan-guhn chuh-kuh-shuh
fire extinguisher	yangın söndürücü	yan-guhn surn-dew-rew-djew
fireworks	havai fişekler	ha-va-ee fee-shek-ler
first	ilk	eelk
the first train	ilk tren	eelk tren
the first bus	ilk otobüs	eelk o-to-bews
first aid	ilk yardım	eelk yar-duhm
first class	birinci sınıf	bee-reen-djee suh-nuhf
first floor	ilk kat	eelk kat
fish	balık	ba-luhk
to fish	balık tutmak	ba-luhk toot-mak
fisherman	balıkçı	ba-luhk-chuh
fishing-rod	olta	ol-ta
fit: *it doesn't fit me*	bana olmadı	ba-na ol-ma-duh

fix: *can you fix it?*	tamir edebilir misiniz?	ta-meer e-de-bee-leer mee-see-neez?
fizzy	köpüklü, gazlı	kur-pewk-lew, gaz-luh
flag	bayrak	bay-rak
flash (for camera)	flaş	fuh-lash
flask	termos	ter-mos
flat (apartment)	daire	da-ee-re
flat	düz	dewz
flavour	tat	tat
flea	pire	pee-re
flight	uçuş	oo-choosh
flood	sel	sel
floor	kat	kat
flour	un	oon
flower	çiçek	chee-chek
flu	grip	guh-reep
fly	sinek	see-nek
to fly	uçmak	ooch-mak
fog	sis	sees
folder	dosya	dos-ya
to follow	takip etmek	ta-keep et-mek
that man is following me	şu adam beni takip ediyor	shoo a-dam be-nee ta-keep e-dee-yor
food	yiyecek	yee-ye-djek
foot	ayak	a-yak
football (game)	futbol	foot-bol
for	için	ee-cheen
for me	benim için	be-neem ee-cheen
for sale	satılık	sa-tuh-luhk
forbidden	yasak	ya-sak
forecast (weather)	hava durumu	ha-va doo-roo- moo
foreign	yabancı	ya-ban-djuh
foreign currency	döviz	dur-veez
forest	orman	or-man
forever	sonsuza dek	son-soo-za dek

to forget	unutmak	oo-noot-mak
I've forgotten my key	anahtarımı unuttum	a-nah-ta-ruh-muh oo-noot-toom
fork (for eating)	çatal	cha-tal
forward(s)	ileri	ee-le-ree
fracture	kırık; çatlak	kuh-ruhk; chat-lak
free (unoccupied)	boş	bosh
(costing nothing)	serbest; bedava	ser-best;be-da-va
freezer	buzluk	booz-look
French	Fransız	fuh-ran-suhz
frequent	sık sık	suhk suhk
fresh	taze	ta-ze
is it fresh?	taze mi?	ta-ze mee?
fresh fruit	taze meyve	ta-ze mey-ve
fresh vegetables	taze sebze	ta-ze seb-ze
fresh milk	taze süt	ta-ze sewt
fresh fish	taze balık	ta-ze ba-luhk
Friday	Cuma	djoo-ma
fridge	buzdolabı	booz-do-la-buh
fried (food)	kızarmış	kuh-zar-mush
friend	arkadaş	ar-ka-dash
from	den/dan	see GRAMMAR
front: *front door*	ön kapı	urn ka-puh
can I sit in the front?	önde oturabilir miyim?	urn-de o-too-ra-bee-leer mee-yeem?
frozen	donmuş	don-moosh
fruit	meyve	mey-ve
fruit juice	meyve suyu	mey-vee soo-yoo
fruit salad	meyve salatası	mey-ve sa-la-ta-suh
fuel	yakıt	ya-kuht
full	dolu	do-loo
full board	tam pansiyon	tam pan-see-yon
furniture	mobilya	mo-beel-ya
further on	ileride	ee-le-ree-de
fuse	sigorta	see-gor-ta
the fuse has blown	sigorta attı	see-gor-ta at-tuh

G

gallery (art)	galeri	ga-le-ree
game (sport)	oyun	o-yoon
(meat)	av eti	av e-tee
garage (private)	garaj	ga-razh
(selling petrol, etc.)	petrol istasyonu	pet-rol ees-tas-yo-noo
garden	bahçe	bah-che
garlic	sarımsak	sar-uhm-sak
gas	gaz	gaz
gate	kapı	ka-puh
gents' toilet	erkek tuvaleti	er-kek too-va-le-tee
genuine	hakiki	ha-kee-kee
is this genuine?	bu hakiki mi?	boo ha-kee-kee mee?
German (nationality)	Alman	al-man
(language)	Almanca	al-man-dja
Germany	Almanya	al-man-ya
to get	almak	al-mak
to get into	girmek	geer-mek
to get on board	binmek	been-mek
to get off (bus, etc.)	inmek	een-mek
gift	hediye	he-dee-ye
gift shop	hediyelik eşya dükkanı	he-dee-ye-leek esh-ya dewk-ka-nuh
girl	kız	kuhz
girlfriend	kız arkadaş	kuzh ar-ka-dash
to give (give back)	vermek	ver-mek
give way	yol ver	yol ver
glass (for drink)	bardak	bar-dak
(substance)	cam	djam
a glass of water	bir bardak su	beer bar-dak soo
a glass of wine	bir bardak şarap	beer bar-dak sha-rap
glasses (spectacles)	gözlük	gurz-lewk
to go	gitmek	geet-mek
goat	keçi	ke-chee

to go back	geri dönmek	ge-ree durn-mek
goggles (for swimming)	deniz gözlüğü	de-neez gurz-lew-ew
to go in	girmek	geer-mek
gold	altın	al-tuhn
golf	golf	golf
golf ball	golf topu	golf to-poo
golf club	golf sopası	golf so-pa-suh
golf course	golf sahası	golf sa-ha-suh
good	iyi	ee-yee
goodbye	hoşçakal	hosh-cha-kal
good day	iyi günler	ee-yee gewn-ler
good evening	iyi akşamlar	ee-yee ak-sham-lar
good morning	günaydın	gew-nay-duhn
goodnight	iyi geceler	ee-yee ge-dje-ler
to go out	çıkmak	chuhk-mak
grandfather	büyükbaba	bew-yewk-ba-ba
grandmother	büyükanne	bew-yewk-an-ne
grapefruit	greyfurt	grey-furt
grapefruit juice	greyfurt suyu	grey-furt soo-yoo
grapes	üzüm	ew-zewm
greasy: *it's too greasy* (food)	çok yağlı	chok ya-luh
Greece	Yunanistan	yoo-na-nees-tan
Greek (language)	Yunanca	yoo-nan-dja
green	yeşil	ye-sheel
greengrocer's	manav	ma-nav
grey	gri	gree
grilled	ızgara	uhz-ga-ra
grocer's	bakkal	bak-kal
group (of people)	grup	goo-roop
guarantee	garanti	ga-ran-tee
guest	misafir	mee-sa-feer
guest-house	pansiyon	pan-see-yon
guide/guidebook	rehber	reh-ber

guided tour	rehberli tur	reh-ber-lee toor
when is the guided tour?	rehberli tur ne zaman?	reh-ber-lee toor ne za-man?

H

hair	saç	sach
hairbrush	saç fırçası	sach fuhr-cha-suh
haircut	saç kestirmek	sach kes-teer-mek
hairdresser	kuaför	koo-a-fur
hair dryer	saç kurutma makinası	sach koo-root-ma ma-kee-na-suh
half	yarım	ya-ruhm
half board	yarım pansiyon	ya-ruhm pan-see-yon
half bottle	yarım şişe	ya-ruhm shee-she
half an hour	yarım saat	ya-ruhm sa-at
ham	jambon	zham-bon
hand	el	el
handbag	el çantası	el chan-ta-suh
hand luggage	el bagajı	el ba-ga-zhuh
hand-made	el yapımı	el ya-puh-muh
to happen	olmak	ol-mak
what happened?	ne oldu?	ne ol-doo?
happy	mutlu	moot-loo
harbour	liman	lee-man
hard (tough)	sert	sert
hat	şapka	shap-ka
hazelnut	fındık	fuhn-duhk
he	o	o
head	baş	bash
headache	baş ağrısı	bash a-ruh-suh
I've got a headache	başım ağrıyor	ba-shuhm a-ruh-yor
to hear	duymak	dooy-mak
hearing aid	işitme cihazı	ee-sheet-me djee-ha-zuh

heart	kalp	kalp
heart attack	kalp krizi	kalp kuh-ree-zee
heating	ısıtıcı	uh-suh-tuh-chu
heavy	ağır	a-uhr
height	yükseklik	yewk-sek-leek
hello	merhaba	mer-ba-ha
help!	imdat!	eem-dat!
to help	yardım etmek	yar-duhm et-mek
can you help me?	yardım edebilir misiniz?	yar-duhm e-der-mee-see-neez?
herbs	baharatlar	ba-ha-rat-laar
here	burada	boo-ra-da
high	yüksek	yewk-sek
high blood pressure	yüksek tansiyon	yewk-sek tan-see-yon
high chair	bebek sandalyesi	be-bek san-dal-ye-see
to hire	kiralamak	kee-ra-la-mak
I want to hire a car	araba kiralamak istiyoruz	a-ra-ba kee-ra-la-mak ees-tee-yo-rooz
to hitch-hike	otostop yapmak	o-to stop yap-mak
holiday	tatil	ta-teel
home	ev	ev
honey	bal	bal
honeymoon	balayı	ba-la-yuh
we're on our honeymoon	balayındayız	ba-la-yuhn-da-yuhz
horse	at	at
hospital	hastane	has-ta-ne
to the hospital, please	hastaneye, lütfen	has-ta-ne-ye, lewt-fen
hot	sıcak	suh-djak
it's too hot	çok sıcak	chok suh-djak
hotel	otel	o-tel
hour	saat	sa-at
in an hour's time	bir saat içinde	beer sa-at ee-cheen-de
house	ev	ev

how?	nasıl?	na-suhl?
how much?	ne kadar?	ne ka-dar?
how many?	kaç tane?	kach ta-ne?
how are you?	nasılsınız?	na-suhl-suh-nuz?
hungry: *I'm hungry*	açım	a-chuhm
hurry: *I'm in a hurry*	acelem var	a-dje-lem var
hurt: *it hurts*	acıyor	a-djuh-yor
husband	eş; koca	esh; ko-ja
my husband	eşim; kocam	e-sheem; ko-djam

I

I	ben	ben
ice	buz	booz
ice cream	dondurma	don-door-ma
iced coffee	buzlu kahve	booz-loo kah-ve
iced tea	buzlu çay	booz-loo chay
iced water	buzlu su	booz-lo soo
identification	kimlik	keem-leek
ill	hasta	has-ta
I'm ill	hastayım	has-ta-yuhm
immediately	hemen	he-men
important	önemli	ur-nem-lee
impossible: *it's impossible*	imkansız	eem-kan-suhz
included	dahil	da-heel
is insurance included?	sigorta dahil mi?	see-gor-ta da-heel-me?
indigestion	hazımsızlık	ha-zuhm-suhz-luhk
infection	enfeksiyon	en-fek-see-yon
information	bilgi	beel-gee
information office	enformasyon bürosu	en-for-mas-yon bew-ro-soo
injured	yaralı	ya-ra-luh
I've been injured	yaralandım	ya-ra-lan-duhm

insect	böcek; haşerat	bur-djek; ha-she-rat
insect bite	böcek ısırması	bur-djek uh-suhr-ma-suh
insect repellent	böcek kovucu	bur-djek ko-voo-djoo
instant coffee	Nescafé®	nes-ka-fe
insurance	sigorta	see-gor-ta
interesting	ilginç	eel-geench
international	uluslararası	oo-loos-lar-a-ra-suh
interpreter	tercüman	ter-djew-man
to invite	davet etmek	da-vet et-mek
invoice	fatura	fa-too-ra
Ireland	İrlanda	eer-lan-da
Irish	İrlandalı	eer-lan-da-luh
iron (metal)	demir	de-meer
(for clothes)	ütü	ew-tew
island	ada	a-da
it	o	o
Italian	İtalyan	ee-tal-yan
Italy	İtalya	ee-tal-ya
itch: it itches	kaşınıyor	ka-shuh-nuh-yor

J

jacket	ceket	dje-ket
leather jacket	deri ceket	de-ree dje-ket
jam (food)	reçel	re-chel
jammed	tıkandı, takıldı	tuh-kan-duh, ta-kuhl-duh
January	Ocak	o-djak
jar	kavanoz	ka-va-noz
jeans	blucin	bloo-djeen
jellyfish	denizanası	de-neez-a-na-suh
jewellery	mücevher	mew-djev-her
Jewish	Yahudi	ya-hoo-dee
I'm Jewish	Yahudiyim	ya-hoo-dee-yeem
job	iş	eesh

183

what's your job?	ne iş yaparsınız?	ne eesh ya-par-suh-nuhz?
joke: it's a joke	bu bir şaka	boo beer sha-ka
journalist	gazeteci	ga-ze-te-djee
journey	seyahat	se-ya-hat
jug	surahi	soo-ra-hee
juice	meyve suyu	mey-ve soo-yoo
orange juice	portakal suyu	por-ta-kal soo-yoo
tomato juice	domates suyu	do-ma-tes soo-yoo
July	Temmuz	tem-mooz
jumper	kazak	ka-zak
junction	kavşak	kav-shak
June	Haziran	ha-zee-ran

K

to keep	saklamak	sak-la-mak
keep the change	üstü kalsın	ews-tew kal-suhn
key	anahtar	a-nah-tar
my key, please	anahtarım, lütfen	a-nah-ta-ruhm, lewt-fen
kind: you're very kind	çok naziksiniz	chok na-zeek-see-neez
to kiss	öpmek	urp-mek
kitchen	mutfak	moot-fak
knee	diz	deez
knife	bıçak	buh-chak
to know	bilmek	beel-mek
I know	biliyorum	bee-lee-yo-room
I don't know	bilmiyorum	beel-mee-yo-room

L

label (luggage)	etiket	e-tee-ket
lace (material)	dantel	dan-tel
laces (for shoes)	bağcık	ba-djuhk
ladies' (toilet)	kadınlar tuvaleti	ka-duhn-lar oo-va-le-tee

184

lager	bira	bee-ra
lake	göl	gurl
lamb	kuzu	koo-zoo
lamp	lamba	lam-ba
land: *has the plane landed?*	uçak indi mi?	oo-chak een-dee mee?
landing	iniş	een-eesh
late	geç	gech
sorry I'm late	üzgünüm geç kaldım	ewz-gew-newm gech kal-duhm
later	daha sonra	da-ha son-ra
launderette	çamaşırhane	cha-ma-shur-ha-ne
laundry service	çamaşır yıkama servisi	cha-ma-shur yuh-ka-ma ser-vee-see
lawyer	avukat	a-voo-kat
leather	deri	de-ree
to leave	ayrılmak; kalkmak	ay-ruhl-mak; kalk-mak
we leave tomorrow	yarın ayrılıyoruz	ya-ruhn ay-ruh-luh-yo-rooz
left	sol	sol
left-luggage office	emanet bürosu	e-ma-net bew-ro-soo
leg	bacak	ba-djak
lemon	limon	lee-mon
lemonade	limonata	le-mo-na-ta
to lend	ödünç vermek	ur-dewnch ver-mek
to let (allow)	izin vermek	ee-zeen ver-mek
licence (driving)	ehliyet	eeh-lee-yet
lifeboat	cankurtaran botu	djan-koor-ta-ran bot-oo
lifeguard	cankurtaran	djan-koor-ta-ran
life jacket	can yeleği	djan ye-le-ee
lift (elevator)	asansör	a-san-sur
light (illumination)	ışık	uh-shuhk
(lamp)	lamba	lam-ba
(not heavy)	hafif	ha-feef

185

do you have a light?	ateşiniz var mı?	a-te-shee-neez var-muh?
light bulb	ampul	am-pool
lighter (cigarette)	çakmak	chak-mak
to like	sevmek	sev-mek
I like coffee	kahve severim	kah-ve se-ve-reem
I don't like coffee	kahve sevmem	kah-ve sev-mem
linen	keten	ke-ten
lipstick	ruj	roozh
to listen to	dinlemek	deen-le-mek
litter (rubbish)	çöp	churp
little (small)	küçük	kew-chewk
just a little, please	biraz, lütfen	bee-raz, lewt-fen
to live	yaşamak	ya-sha-mak
I live in London	Londra'da oturuyorum	lond-ra-da o-too-roo-yo-room
lock	kilit	kee-leet
to lock	kilitlemek	kee-leet-le-mek
locker (for luggage)	kilitli dolap	ke-leet-lee do-lap
long	uzun	oo-zoon
how long will it take?	ne kadar sürer?	ne ka-dar sew-rer?
to look after someone	bakmak	bak-mak
to look for	aramak	a-ra-mak
lorry	kamyon	kam-yon
lost	kayıp	ka-yuhp
lost property office	kayıp eşya bürosu	ka-yuhp esh-ya bew-ro-soo
lot: a lot	çok	chok
lotion	losyon	los-yon
loud	yüksek sesle	yewk-sek ses-le
to love	sevmek	sev-mek
I love you	seni seviyorum	se-nee se-vee-yo-room
lovely	güzel	gew-zel

lucky	şanslı	shans-luh
luggage	bagaj	ba-gazh
lunch	öğle yemeği	uur-le ye-me-ee

M

maid	hizmetçi	heez-met-chee
main course (of meal)	ana yemek	a-na ye-mek
to make	yapmak	yap-mak
man	adam	a-dam
manager	müdür	mew-dewr
map	harita	ha-ree-ta
marble	mermer	mer-mer
March	Mart	mart
marmalade	marmelat	mar-me-lat
married	evli	ev-lee
I'm married	evliyim	ev-lee-yeem
I'm not married	evli değilim	ev-lee de-ee-leem
are you married?	evli misiniz?	ev-lee mee-see-neez?
match (game)	maç	mach
matches (light)	kibrit	keeb-reet
maximum speed	azami hız	a-za-mee huhz
May	Mayıs	ma-yuhs
meal	yemek	ye-e-mek
mean: *what does it mean?*	o ne demek?	o ne de-mek?
measure: *can I measure it?*	ölçebilir miyim?	url-che-bee-leer mee-yeem?
meat	et	et
meatball	köfte	kurf-te
medicine	ilaç	ee-lach
to meet	buluşmak	boo-loosh-mak
meeting	toplantı	top-lan-tuh
to mend	onarmak; tamir etmek	o-nar-mak; ta-meer et-mek

187

menu	menü; yemek listesi	mee-new;ye-mek lees-te-see
the menu, please	menü, lütfen	me-new, lewt-fen
message	mesaj	me-sazh
are there any messages?	bana mesaj var mı?	ba-na me-sazh var muh?
meter (taxi)	taksimetre	tak-see-met-re
metre	metre	met-re
microwave (oven)	mikrodalga fırın	meek-ro-dal-ga fuh-ruhn
midday	öğlen	ur-len
middle	orta	or-ta
midnight	gece yarısı	ge-dje ya-ruh-suh
milk	süt	sewt
mince (meat)	kıyma	kuhy-ma
mineral water	maden suyu	ma-den soo-yoo
mints	nane	na-ne
minute	dakika	da-kee-ka
mirror	ayna	ay-na
miss (plane, train, etc.)	kaçırmak	ka-chuhr-mak
I missed the bus	otobüsü kaçırdım	o-to-bew-sew ka-chuhr-duhm
missing (thing)	kayıp	ka-yuhp
my wallet is missing	cüzdanım kayıp	djewz-da-nuhm ka-yuhp
mistake	hata; yanlışlık	ha-ta; yan-luhsh-luhk
monastery	manastır	ma-nas-tuhr
Monday	Pazartesi	pa-zar-te-see
money	para	pa-ra
month	ay	ay
monument	anıt	a-nuht
moon	ay	ay
more	daha	da-ha
some more...	biraz daha…	bee-raz da-ha…
more bread, please	biraz daha ekmek, lütfen	bee-raz da-ha ek-mek, lewt-fen

morning	sabah	sa-bah
in the morning	sabahleyin	sa-bah-le-yeen
tomorrow morning	yarın sabah	ya-ruhn sa-bah
this morning	bu sabah	boo sa-bah
mosque	cami	dja-mee
mosquito net	cibinlik	djee-been-leek
mosquitoes	sivrisinekler	seev-ree-see-nek-ler
mother	anne	an-ne
mother-in-law	kayınvalide	ka-yuhn-va-lee-de
motorbike	motorsiklet	mo-to-seek-let
motorway	otoyol	o-to-yol
mountain	dağ	da
mouse	fare	fa-re
moustache	bıyık	buh-yuhk
mouth	ağız	a-uhz
much	çok	chok
how much?	ne kadar?	ne ka-dar?
too much	çok fazla	chok faz-la
it's too much (too expensive)	çok pahalı	chok pa-ha-luh
museum	müze	mew-ze
Muslim	müslüman	mews-lew-man
mussels	midye	meed-ye
mustard	hardal	har-dal

N

nail (metal)	çivi	chee-vee
(finger, toe)	tırnak	tuhr-nak
nail polish	oje	o-zhe
nail polish remover	aseton	a-se-ton
name	ad; isim	ad; ee-seem
my name is...	ismim...	ees-meem...
what's your name?	isminiz nedir?	ees-mee-neez ne?
napkin	peçete	pe-che-te

nappy	çocuk bezi	cho-djook be-zee
narrow	dar	dar
nationality	milliyet	meel-lee-yet
navy blue	lacivert	la-djee-vert
near	yakın	ya-kuhn
is it near?	yakın mı?	ya-kuhn muh?
necessary	gerekli	ge-rek-lee
is it necessary to book?	rezervasyon gerekli mi?	re-zer-vas-yon ge-rek-lee-mee?
neck	boyun	bo-yoon
to need	ihtiyacı olmak	eeh-tee-ya-djuh ol-mak
I need...	...ihtiyacım var	...eeh-tee-ya-djuhm var
I need a car	arabaya ihtiyacım var	a-ra-ba-ya eeh-tee-ya-djuhm var
I need to go	gitmem gerek	geet-mem ge-rek
needle	iğne	ee-neh
a needle and thread	iğne ve iplik	ee-ne ve eep-leek
neighbour	komşu	kom-shoo
nephew	yeğen	ye-en
never	asla	as-la
new	yeni	ye-nee
news	haberler	ha-ber-ler
newspaper	gazete	ga-ze-te
an English newspaper	bir İngilizce gazete	beer en-gee-lez-dje ga-ze-te
newsstand	gazete bayii	ga-ze-te ba-yee-ee
New Year	Yeni yıl	ye-nee yuhl
New Zealand	Yeni Zelanda	ye-nee ze-lan-da
next	bir sonraki	beer son-ra-kee
when is the next boat?	bir sonraki vapur saat kaçta?	beer son-ra-kee va-poor sa-at kach-ta?
when is the next bus?	bir sonraki otobüs saat kaçta?	beer son-ra-kee o-to-bews sa-at kach-ta?

next to	yanında	ya-nuhn-da
nice	hoş	hosh
it's very nice	çok hoş	chok hosh
we had a very nice time	çok hoş vakit geçirdik	chok hosh va-keet ge-cheer-deek
niece	yeğen	ye-en
night	gece	ge-dje
last night	dün gece	dewn ge-dje
nightclub	gece klübü	ge-dje klew-bew
no	hayır	ha-yuhr
no, thanks	hayır teşekkürler	ha-yuhr te-shek-kewr-ler
noisy	gürültülü	gew-rewl-tew-lew
non-alcoholic	alkolsüz	al-kol-sewz
a non-alcoholic drink	alkolsüz bir içecek	al-kol-sewz beer ee-che-djek
none	hiç	heech
there's none left	hiç kalmadı	heech kal-ma-duh
non-smoking	sigara içilmez	see-ga-ra ee-cheel-mez
north	kuzey	koo-zey
Northern Ireland	Kuzey İrlanda	koo-zey eer-lan-da
I'm from Northern Ireland	Kuzey İrlandalıyım	koo-zey eer-lan-da-luh-yuhm
nose	burun	boo-roon
not	değil	de-eel
notebook	not defteri	not def-te-ree
nothing	hiçbirşey	heech-beer-shey
November	Kasım	ka-suhm
now	şimdi	sheem-dee
number	numara	noo-ma-ra
phone number	telefon numarası	te-le-fon noo-ma-ra-suh
number plate	plaka	puh-la-ka
nurse	hemşire	hem-shee-re
nuts (bar nibbles)	çerez	che-rez

O

October	Ekim	e-keem
octopus	ahtapot	ah-ta-pot
off (radio, engine, etc.)	kapalı	ka-pa-luh
the heating is off	kalorifer kapalı	ka-loh-ree-fer ka-pa-luh
this is off (milk, food)	bu bozulmuş	boo bo-zool-moosh
office	ofis; büro	o-fees; bew-ro
I work in an office	bir ofiste çalışıyorum	beer o-fees-de cha-luh-shuh-yo-room
often	sık sık	suhk suhk
oil	yağ	ya
OK	tamam; peki	ta-mam; pe-kee
old (person)	yaşlı	yash-luh
(thing)	eski	es-kee
how old are you?	kaç yaşındasınız?	kach ya-shuhn-da-suh-nuhz?
I'm ... years old	…yaşındayım	…ya-shuhn-da-yuhm
how old is it? (building, etc.)	ne kadar eski?	ne ka-dar es-kee?
olive oil	zeytinyağı	zey-teen ya-uh
olives	zeytin	zey-teen
on	üzerinde	ew-ze-reen-de
once: *at once*	hemen	he-men
one	bir	beer
onion	soğan	so-an
only: *only one*	sadece bir tane	sa-de-dje beer ta-ne
open	açık	a-chuhk
is it open?	açık mı?	a-chuhk muh?
to open	açmak	ach-mak
opening hours	mesai saatleri	me-sa-ee sa-at-le-ree
operator (telephone)	operatör	o-pe-ra-tur
opposite	karşısında	kar-shuh-suhn-da

optician	gözlükçü	gurz-lewk-chew
or	veya	ve-ya
orange (colour)	turuncu	too-roon-djoo
orange	portakal	por-ta-kal
orange juice	portakal suyu	por-ta-kal soo-yoo
orchestra	orkestra	or-kes-tra
to order (food)	ısmarlamak	uhs-mar-la-mak
other	diğer	dee-er
our	bizim	bee-zeem
out	dışında	duh-shuhn-da
he's gone out	dışarıya çıktı	duh-sha-ruh-ya chuhk-tuh
out of order	bozuk	bo-zook
oven	fırın	fuh-ruhn
to overtake	geçmek	gech-mek
to owe	borcu olmak	bor-djoo ol-mak
you owe me 10 lira	bana 10 lira borcun var	ba-na 10 lee-ra bor-joon var
what do I owe you?	sana ne kadar borcum var?	sa-na ne ka-dar bor-djoom var?
owner	sahip; patron	sa-heep; pat-ron

P

to pack (bags)	toplamak	top-la-mak
package tour	paket tur	pa-ket toor
packet	paket	pa-ket
paid: I've already paid	zaten ödedim	za-ten ur-de-deem
painful: it's very painful	çok acı verici	chok a-djuh ve-ree-djee
painkiller	ağrı kesici	a-ruh ke-see-djee
painting (picture)	resim; tablo	re-seem; tab-lo
pair	çift	cheeft
palace	saray	sa-ray
pancake	krep	krep
pants (trousers)	pantolon	pan-to-lon

paper	kağıt	ka-uht
parcel	koli; paket	ko-lee; pa-ket
parcels counter	koli gişesi	ko-lee gee-she-see
pardon!	pardon!	par-don!
parents	anne-baba	an-ne ba-ba
park	park	park
to park	park etmek	park et-mek
part (spare)	yedek parça	ye-dek par-cha
partner (business)	ortak	or-tak
my partner (in couple)	eşim	e-sheem
party (celebration)	parti	par-tee
passenger	yolcu	yol-djoo
passport	pasaport	pa-sa-port
passport control	pasaport kontrolü	pa-sa-port kon-tro-lew
pasta	makarna	ma-kar-na
pastry (cake)	pasta	pas-ta
to pay	ödemek	ur-de-mek
where do I pay?	nereye ödeyebilirim?	ne-re-ye ur-de-ye-bee-lee-reem?
peanuts	yerfıstığı	yer fuhs-tuh-uh
pearl	inci	een-djee
pedestrian	yaya	ya-ya
pedestrian crossing	yaya geçidi	ya-ya ge-chee-dee
peg: *clothes peg*	mandal	man-dal
pen	kalem	ka-lem
pencil	kurşun kalem	koor-shoon ka-lem
penicillin	penisilin	pe-nee-see-leen
pensioner	emekli	e-mek-lee
pepper (spice)	karabiber	ka-ra-bee-ber
(vegetables)	biber	bee-ber
per	başı	ba-shuh
per hour	saat başı	sa-at ba-shuh
per week	hafta başı	haf-ta ba-shuh

per kilometre	kilometre başı	ki-lo-met-re ba-shuh
perfect: *it's perfect*	mükemmel	mew-kem-mel
performance	gösteri; temsil	gurs-te-ree; tem-seel
perfume	parfüm	par-fewm
permit: *do I need a permit?*	izin almalı mıyım?	ee-zeen al-ma-luh muh-yuhm?
person	kişi	kee-shee
per person	kişi başı	kee-shee ba-shuh
petrol	benzin	ben-zeen
unleaded petrol	kurşunsuz benzin	koor-shoon-sooz ben-zeen
petrol station	benzin istasyonu	ben-zeen ees-tas-yo-noo
phone	telefon	te-le-fon
phonecard	telefon kartı	te-le-fon kar-tuh
photocopy	fotokopi	fo-to-ko-pee
photograph	fotoğraf	fo-to-raf
picnic	piknik	peek-neek
picture (on wall)	resim; tablo	re-seem; tab-lo
pie	börek	bur-rek
piece (slice)	dilim	dee-leem
pier	iskele; rıhtım	ees-ke-le; ruh-tuhm
pill	hap	hap
pillow	yastık	yas-tuhk
pin	toplu iğne	top-loo ee-ne
pink	pembe	pem-be
pipe (for smoking)	pipo	pee-po
(drain, etc.)	boru	bo-roo
plain	sade	sa-de
plane	uçak	oo-chak
plaster	yara bandı	ya-ra ban-duh
plastic	plastik	puh-las-teek
plate	tabak	ta-bak
platform (railway)	peron	pe-ron
which platform?	hangi peron?	han-gee pe-ron?

to play	oynamak	oy-na-mak
please	lütfen	lewt-fen
plug (electric)	fiş	feesh
(for sink)	tıkaç	tuh-kach
plumber	muslukçu	moos-look-choo
pocket	cep	djep
poisonous	zehirli	ze-heer-lee
police	polis	po-lees
police station	karakol, polis istasyonu	ka-ra-kol, po-les es-tas-yo-noo
polish (for shoes)	cilalamak	djee-la-la-mak
pool	havuz	ha-vooz
is there a pool?	havuz var mı?	ha-vooz var-muh?
poor (not rich)	fakir	fa-keer
pork	domuz eti	do-mooz e-tee
port (harbour)	liman	lee-man
porter (for door)	kapıcı	ka-puh-djuh
(for luggage)	hamal	ha-mal
possible	mümkün	mewm-kewn
to post	postalamak	pos-ta-la-mak
postbox	posta kutusu	pos-ta koo-too-soo
postcard	kartpostal	kart-pos-tal
postcode	posta kodu	pos-ta ko-doo
poster	afiş	a-feesh
post office	postane	pos-ta-ne
where is the post office?	postane nerede?	pos-ta-ne ne-re-de?
pot (for cooking)	tencere	ten-dje-re
potato	patates	pa-ta-tes
boiled potatoes	haşlanmış patates	hash-lan-mush pa-ta-tes
fried potatoes	kızarmış patates	kuh-zar-mush pa-ta-tes
mashed potato	patates püresi	pa-ta-tes pew-re-see
potato salad	patates salatası	pa-ta-tes sa-la-ta-suh
powdered milk	süt tozu	sewt to-zoo

prawns	karides	ka-ree-des
prayers	namaz	na-maz
to prefer	tercih etmek	ter-djeeh et-mek
I'd prefer tea	çay tercih ederim	chay ter-djeeh e-de-reem
pregnant	hamile	ha-mee-le
I'm pregnant	hamileyim	ha-mee-le-yeem
prescription	reçete	re-che-te
present (gift)	hediye	he-dee-ye
this is a present	bu bir hediyedir	boo beer he-dee-ye-deer
pretty	hoş	hosh
price	fiyat	fee-yat
price list	fiyat listesi	fee-yat lees-te-see
private	özel	ur-zel
private bathroom	özel banyo	ur-zel ban-yo
probably	galiba	ga-lee-ba
to pronounce	telaffuz etmek	te-laf-fooz et-mek
how is this pronounced?	bu nasıl telaffuz ediliyor?	boo na-suhl te-laf-fooz e-dee-lee-yor?
public holiday	resmi tatil	res-mee ta-teel
pudding	tatlı	tat-luh
to pull	çekmek	chek-mek
purple	mor	mor
to push	itmek	et-mek
pushchair	puset	poo-set
pyjamas	pijama	pee-zha-ma

Q

quality	kalite	ka-lee-te
good quality	iyi kalite	ee-yee ka-lee-te
poor quality	kötü kalite	kur-tew ka-lee-te
quay	rıhtım; iskele	ruh-tuhm; ees-ke-le
queen	kraliçe	kuh-ra-lee-che
question	soru	so-roo

queue	kuyruk	kooy-rook
to queue	kuyruk olmak	kooy-rook ol-mak
quickly	çabuk	cha-book
quiet	sessiz; sakin	ses-seez; sa-keen
quilt	yorgan	yor-gan

R

rabbit	tavşan	tav-shan
rabies	kuduz	koo-dooz
race (sport)	yarış	ya-rush
radio	radyo	rad-yo
radish	turp	toorp
railway	demiryolu	de-meer-yo-loo
railway station	tren istasyonu; tren garı	tren ees-tas-yo-noo; tren ga-ruh
rain	yağmur	ya-moor
raincoat	yağmurluk	ya-moor-look
raisins	kuru üzüm	koo-roo ew-zewm
rare (steak)	az pişmiş	az peesh-meesh
rash (skin)	isilik	ee-see-leek
rat	sıçan	suh-chan
rate: *exchange rate*	döviz kuru	dur-veez koo-roo
raw	ham; çiğ	ham; chee
razor	jilet	zhee-let
to read (book, etc.)	okumak	o-koo-mak
ready	hazır	ha-zuhr
is it ready?	hazır mı?	ha-zuhr-muh?
real	hakiki	ha-kee-kee
is it real leather?	bu hakiki deri mi?	boo ha-kee-kee de-ree mee?
is it real gold?	bu hakiki altın mı?	boo ha-kee-kee al-tuhn muh?
receipt	makbuz; fiş	mak-booz; feesh
reception (desk)	resepsiyon	re-sep-see-yon

recipe	yemek tarifi	ye-mek ta-ree-fee
to recommend	tavsiye etmek	tav-see-ye et-mek
red	kırmızı	kuhr-muh-zuh
red wine	kırmızı şarap	kuhr-muh-zuh sha-rap
reduction	indirim	een-dee-reem
to refund	geri ödemek	gee-re uh-de-mek
I'd like a refund	paramı geri ödermisiniz	pa-ra-muh ge-ree ur-der-mee-see-neez
regulations	kurallar	koo-ral-lar
relation (family member)	akraba	ak-ra-ba
reliable (person, service)	güvenilir	gew-ve-nee-leer
to remember	hatırlamak	ha-tuhr-la-mak
rent	kira	kee-ra
how much is the rent?	kirası ne kadar?	kee-ra-suh ne ka-dar?
to rent	kiralamak	kee-ra-la-mak
to repair	onarmak	o-nar-mak
to repeat	tekrar etmek	tek-rar et-mek
reservation	rezervasyon	re-zer-vas-yon
to reserve (room, table, etc.)	rezerve etmek	re-zer-ve et-mek
reserved	ayrılmış	ay-ruhl-muhsh
to rest	dinlenmek	deen-len-mek
I need to rest	dinlenmeye ihtiyacım var	deen-len-me-ye eeh-tee-ya-djuhm var
restaurant	lokanta; restoran	lo-kan-ta; res-to-ran
retired	emekli	e-mek-lee
to return	dönmek	durn-mek
return (ticket)	gidiş-dönüş	gee-deesh dur-newsh
reverse-charge call	ödemeli görüşme	ur-de-me-lee gur-rewsh-me
rice (cooked)	pilav	pee-lav
(uncooked)	pirinç	pee-reench

rich (person)	zengin	zen-geen
(food)	ağır	a-uhr
right (correct)	doğru	do-roo
(not left)	sağ	sa
on/to the right	sağda/sağa	sa-da/sa-a
ring (for finger)	yüzük	yew-zewk
river	nehir	ne-heer
road	yol	yol
is this the road to Izmir?	İzmir'e giden yol bu mu?	eez-meer-e gee-den yol boo moo?
road map	yol haritası	yol ha-ree-ta-suh
roof	çatı	cha-tuh
room	oda	o-da
room service	oda servisi	o-da ser-vee-see
rope	halat	ha-lat
rose	gül	gewl
rotten (food)	çürük	chew-rewk
route	güzergâh	gew-zer-gaah
what's the best route?	en iyi güzergâh hangisi?	en ee-yee gew-zer-gaah han-gee-see?
rowing boat	sandal; kayık	san-dal; ka-yuhk
rubber	lastik	las-teek
rubbish	çöp	churp
rucksack	sırt çantası	suhrt chan-ta-suh
rug	kilim	kee-leem

S

sad	üzgün	ewz-gewn
safe (for valuables)	kasa	ka-sa
safe (medicine etc.)	güvenli	gew-ven-lee
is it safe to swim?	yüzmek için güvenli mi?	yewz-mek e-cheen gew-ven-lee mee?
safety pin	çengelli iğne	chen-gel-lee ee-ne
sailing	yelken yapmak	yel-ken yap-mak

sale	indirimli satışlar	een-dee-reem-lee sa-tuhsh-lar
for sale	satılık	sa-tuh-luhk
salad	salata	sa-la-ta
salesperson	satıcı	sa-tuh-djuh
salmon	somon balığı	so-mon ba-luh-uh
salt	tuz	tooz
same	aynı	ay-nuh
sand	kum	koom
sandals	sandalet	san-da-let
sanitary towel	kadın bağı	ka-duhn ba-uh
sardines	sardalye	sar-dal-ye
Saturday	Cumartesi	djoo-mar-te-see
sauce	sos	sos
saucepan	saplı tencere	sap-luh ten-dje-re
sausage	sosis	so-sees
savoury	tuzlu	tooz-loo
to say	söylemek	suy-le-mek
what did you say?	ne dediniz?	nee de-dee-neez?
please say that again	tekrar eder misiniz, lütfen	tek-rar e-der mee-see-neez, lewt-fen
school	okul	o-kool
scissors	makas	ma-kas
scorpion	akrep	ak-rep
Scotland	İskoçya	ees-koch-ya
Scottish	İskoçyalı	ees-koch-ya-luh
I'm Scottish	İskoçyalıyım	ees-koch-ya-luh-yuhm
sculpture	heykel	hey-kel
sea	deniz	de-neez
seafood	deniz ürünleri	de-nez ew-rewn-le-ree
seasick: *I'm feeling seasick*	beni deniz tuttu	be-nee de-neez toot-too
seat (chair)	sandalye	san-dal-ye
(on bus, train, etc.)	yer	yer
reserved seat	ayrılmış yer	ay-ruhl-muhsh yer

201

seat belt	emniyet kemeri	em-nee-yet ke-me-ree
second	ikinci	ee-keen-djee
second-class	ikinci sınıf	ee-keen-djee suh-nuhf
a second-class ticket	bir ikinci sınıf bilet	beer ee-keen-djee suh-nuhf bee-let
secondhand	ikinci el	ee-keen-djee el
to see	görmek	gur-mek
to sell	satmak	sat-mak
to send	göndermek	gurn-der-mek
senior citizen	yaşlı vatandaş	yash-luh va-tan-dash
separate	ayrı	ay-ruh
separately	ayrı ayrı	ay-ruh ay-ruh
September	Eylül	ey-lewl
serious	ciddi	djeed-dee
is it serious?	ciddi mi?	djeed-dee mee?
service	servis	ser-vees
service charge	servis ücreti	ser-vees ewdj-re-tee
set menu	fiks menü	feeks me-new
shade (shadow)	gölge	gurl-ge
shallow (water)	sığ	suh
shampoo	şampuan	sham-poo-an
to shave	traş olmak	tuh-rash ol-mak
shaver	elektrikli traş makınası	e-lek-treek-lee tuh-rash ma-kee-na-suh
shaver socket	traş makınası için priz	tuh-rash ma-kee-na-suh ee-cheen preez
shaving cream	traş kremi	tuh-rash kuh-re-mee
she	o	o
sheep	koyun	ko-yoon
sheet (for bed)	çarşaf	char-shaf
shelf	raf	raf
shell	kabuk	ka-book
shellfish	kabuklu deniz ürünleri	ka-book-loo de-neez ew-rewn-le-ree

I don't eat shellfish	kabuklu deniz ürünü yemem	ka-book-loo de-neez ew-rew-new ye-mem
ship	vapur; gemi	va-poor; ge-mee
shirt	gömlek	gurm-lek
shoes	ayakkabı	a-yak-ka-buh
shop	dükkan	dewk-kan
shop assistant	tezgâhtar	tez-gah-tar
shopping	alışveriş	a-luhsh ve-reesh
short	kısa	kuh-sa
shorts (short trousers)	şort	short
show	gösteri	gurs-te-ree
to show	göstermek	gurs-ter-mek
shower (bath)	duş	doosh
shrimps	karides	ka-ree-des
shut	kapalı	ka-pa-luh
to shut	kapatmak	ka-pat-mak
sick: *I feel sick*	midem bulanıyor	mee-dem boo-la-nuh-yor
sightseeing	gezip-görmek	ge-zeep gur-mek
sign (road-, notice, etc.)	tabela	ta-be-la
to sign (form, cheque, etc.)	imzalamak	eem-za-la-mak
signature	imza	eem-za
silk	ipek	ee-pek
is it silk?	ipek mi?	ee-pek mee?
silver	gümüş	gew-mewsh
is it silver?	gümüş mü?	gew-mewsh mew?
simple (easy)	basit	ba-seet
(unadorned)	sade	sa-de
single (lone)	tek	tek
(ticket)	tek yön bilet	tek yurn bee-let
(unmarried)	bekar	be-kar
I'm single	bekarım	be-ka-ruhm
single room	tek kişilik oda	tek kee-shee-leek o-da

sink	lavabo	la-va-bo
sister	kız kardeş	kuhz kar-desh
sit	oturmak	o-toor-mak
size	beden	be-den
(shoes)	ayakkabı numarası	a-yak-ka-buh noo-ma-ra-suh
bigger size	daha büyük beden	da-ha bew-yewk be-den
smaller size	daha küçük beden	da-ha kew-chewk be-den
to skate	paten yapmak	pa-ten yap-mak
skates	paten	pa-ten
skiing	kayak	ka-yak
skimmed milk	yağsız süt	ya-suhz sewt
skin	deri	de-ree
skirt	etek	e-tek
sky	gökyüzü	gurk-yew-zew
to sleep	uyumak	oo-yoo-mak
sleeping bag	uyku tulumu	ooy-koo too-loo-moo
sleeping pill	uyku ilacı	ooy-koo ee-la-djuh
slice	dilim	dee-leem
slippers	terlik	ter-leek
slow	yavaş	ya-vash
small	küçük	kew-chewk
smaller	daha küçük	da-ha kew-chewk
smell	koku	ko-koo
to smell	koklamak	kok-la-mak
smile	gülümsemek	gew-lewm-se-mek
smoke	duman	doo-man
to smoke	sigara içmek	see-ga-ra eech-mek
I don't smoke	sigara içmiyorum	see-ga-ra eech-mee-yo-room
please don't smoke	lütfen sigara içmeyin	lewt-fen see-ga-ra eech-me-yeen
snake	yılan	yuh-lan
snorkelling	şnorkelle dalmak	shnor-kel-le dal-mak

snow	kar	kar
soap	sabun	sa-boon
socket (electrical)	priz	pee-reez
socks	kısa-çorap	kuh-sa cho-rap
soft	yumuşak	yoo-moo-shak
soft drink	meşrubat	mesh-roo-bat
sold out	satıldı, bitti	sa-tul-duh, beet-tee
some	biraz	bee-raz
someone	birisi	bee-ree-see
something	birşey	beer-shey
sometimes	bazen	ba-zen
son	oğul	o-ool
song	şarkı	shar-kuh
soon	yakında	ya-kuhn-da
sorry: *I'm sorry!*	üzgünüm!	ewz-gew-newm!
sort (type)	çeşit	che-sheet
soup	çorba	chor-ba
south	güney	gew-ney
souvenir	hediyelik eşya	he-dee-ye-leek esh-ya
souvenir shop	hediyelik eşya satan dükkan	he-dee-ye-leek esh-ya sa-tan dewk-kan
sparkling	köpüklü	kur-pewk-lew
to speak	konuşmak	ko-noosh-mak
do you speak English?	İngilizce biliyor musunuz?	een-gee-leez-dje bee-lee-yor-moo-soo-nooz?
I don't speak Turkish	Türkçe bilmiyorum	tewrk-che beel-mee-yo-room
special	özel	ur-zel
speed	hız	huhz
spell: *how do you spell it?*	nasıl yazılıyor?	na-suhl ya-zuh-luh-yor?
spice	baharat	ba-ha-rat
spicy	baharatlı	ba-ha-rat-luh
spirits	alkollü içkiler	al-kol-lew eech-kee-ler

205

sponge (for cleaning)	sünger	sewn-ger
spoon	kaşık	ka-shuhk
sport	spor	spor
spring (season)	ilkbahar	eelk-ba-har
square (in town)	meydan	mey-dan
squid	kalamar	ka-la-mar
stadium	stadyum	stad-yoom
stairs	merdiven	mer-dee-ven
stamp	pul	pool
star	yıldız	yuhl-duhz
to start	başlamak	bash-la-mak
when does it start?	ne zaman başlıyor?	ne za-man bash-luh-yor?
station	istasyon; gar	ees-tas-yon; gar
bus station	otobüs terminali; otogar	o-to-bews ter-mee-na-lee; o-to-gar
train station	tren garı	tren ga-ruh
to stay	kalmak	kal-mak
I'm staying at the ... Hotel	Otel ... 'de/da kalıyorum	o-tel ... de/da ka-luh-yo-room
steep: is it steep?	yokuş yukarı mı?	yo-koosh yoo-ka-ruh muh?
still (not fizzy)	köpüksüz	kur-pewk-sewz
to sting (bite)	sokmak	sok-mak
(burn)	yakmak	yak-mak
wasp sting	arı sokması	a-ruh sok-ma-suh
stomach	mide	mee-de
stop!	dur!	door!
storm	fırtına	fuhr-tuh-na
straight on	düz	dewz
keep straight on	düz gidin	dewz gee-deen
straw (for drinking)	kamış	ka-mush
street	sokak	so-kak
(major road)	cadde	djad-de
street map	sokak haritası	so-kak ha-ree-ta-suh

string	ip; sicim	eep; see-djeem
strong (tea, coffee)	koyu	ko-yoo
stuck: *it's stuck*	yapışmış	ya-puhsh-mush
student	öğrenci	ur-ren-djee
stung: *I've been stung by a bee*	beni bir arı soktu	be-nee beer a-ruh sok-too
stupid	aptal	ap-tal
suede	süet	sew-et
sugar	şeker	she-ker
suit (clothes)	takım elbise	ta-kuhm el-bee-se
suitcase	valiz; bavul	va-leez; ba-vool
I've lost my suitcase	bavulumu kaybettim	ba-voo-loo-moo kay-bet-teem
summer	yaz	yaz
in summer	yazın	ya-zuhn
sun	güneş	gew-nesh
sunbathe	güneşlenmek	gew-nesh-len-mek
sunburn	güneş yanığı	gew-nesh ya-nuh-uh
Sunday	Pazar	pa-zar
sunglasses	güneş gözlüğü	gew-nesh gurz-lew-ew
sunshade	güneşlik	gew-nesh-leek
sunstroke	güneş çarpması	gew-nesh charp-ma-suh
suntan lotion	güneş kremi	gew-nesh kuh-re-mee
supermarket	süpermarket	sew-per-mar-ket
supplement	ilave	ee-la-ve
surfboard	sörf tahtası	surf tah-ta-suh
surfing	sörf yapmak	surf yap-mak
surname	soyadı	so-ya-duh
sweater	kazak	ka-zak
sweet	tatlı	tat-luh
sweetener	sakarin	sa-ka-reen
sweets	şekerleme	she-ker-le-me
to swim	yüzmek	yewz-mek
swimming-pool	yüzme havuzu	yewz-me ha-voo-zoo

is there a swimming-pool?	yüzme havuzu var mı?	yewz-me ha-voo-zoo var-muh?
swimsuit	mayo	ma-yo
switch	elektrik düğmesi	el-lek-treek dew-me-see
to switch off	kapatmak	ka-pat-mak
to switch on	açmak	ach-mak
swollen (finger, ankle, etc.)	şişmiş	sheesh-meesh

T

table	masa	ma-sa
table tennis	masa tenisi	ma-sa te-nee-see
to take	almak	al-mak
can I take pictures?	fotoğraf çekebilir miyim?	fo-to-raf che-ke-bee-leer mee-yeem?
will you take a picture of us?	fotoğrafımızı çekebilir misiniz?	fo-to-ra-fuh-muh-zuh che-ke-bee-leer? mee-see-neez
to talk	konuşmak	ko-noosh-mak
tall	uzun	oo-zoon
tap	musluk	moos-look
tape (cassette)	kaset	ka-set
taste: *can I taste some?*	biraz tadabilir miyim?	bee-raz ta-da-bee-leer mee-yeem?
tasty	lezzetli	lez-zet-lee
tax	vergi	ver-gee
taxi	taksi	tak-see
tea	çay	chay
tea bag	poşet çay	po-shet chay
teacher	öğretmen	ur-ret-men
team (football, etc.)	takım	ta-kuhm
teeth	dişler	deesh-ler
telephone	telefon	te-le-fon
to telephone	telefon etmek	te-le-fon et-mek

can I telephone from here?	buradan telefon edebilir miyim?	boo-ra-dan te-le-fon e-de-bee-leer-mee-yeem?
telephone box	telefon kulübesi	te-le-fon koo-lew-be-see
telephone call	telefon görüşmesi	te-le-fon gur-rewsh-me-see
international telephone call	uluslararası telefon görüşmesi	oo-loos-lar-a-ra-suh te-le-fon gur-rewsh-me-see
telephone directory	telefon rehberi	te-le-fon reh-be-ree
television	televizyon	te-le-veez-yon
temperature	ısı	uh-suh
(fever)	ateş	a-tesh
I have a temperature	ateşim var	a-te-sheem var
what is the temperature?	hava sıcaklığı kaç?	ha-va suh-djak-luh-uh kach?
temporary	geçici	ge-chee-djee
tennis	tenis	te-nees
I'd like to play tennis	tenis oynamak istiyorum	te-nees oy-na-mak ees-tee-yo-room
do you play tennis?	tenis oynar mısınız?	te-nees oy-nar muh-su-nuz?
tennis ball	tenis topu	te-nees to-poo
tennis court	tenis kortu	te-nees kor-too
tennis racket	tenis raketi	te-nees ra-ke-tee
tent	çadır	cha-duhr
terrace	teras	te-ras
tetanus	tetanoz	te-ta-noz
thanks	teşekkürler	te-shek-kewr-ler
thank you	teşekkür ederim	te-shek-kewre-de-reem
that	o; şu	o; shoo
theatre	tiyatro	tee-yat-ro

there: there is.../ there are...	...var	...var
is there...?	...var mı?	...var muh?
these	bunlar	boon-lar
they	onlar	on-lar
thief	hırsız	huhr-suhz
thin	ince	een-dje
to think	sanmak	san-mak
I think so	sanırım	sa-nuh-ruhm
I don't think so	sanmıyorum	san-muh-yo-room
thirsty: I'm thirsty	susadım	soo-sa-duhm
this	bu	boo
those	şunlar	shoon-lar
thread	iplik	eep-leek
Thursday	Perşembe	per-shem-be
ticket	bilet	bee-let
single ticket	tek yön bilet	tek yurn bee-let
return ticket	gidiş-dönüş bilet	gee-deesh dur-newsh bee-let
ticket office	gişe	gee-she
tie	kravat	kra-vat
tight: it's too tight	çok sıkı; çok dar	chok suh-kuh;chok dar
tights	külotlu çorap	kew-lot-loo cho-rap
time	zaman	za-man
timetable	tarife	ta-ree-fe
tin-opener	konserve açacağı	kon-ser-ve a-cha-dja-uh
tip (to waiter, etc.)	bahşiş	bah-sheesh
tired	yorgun	yor-goon
tissues	kağıt mendil	ka-uht men-deel
to	-ye/ya/e/a;	see GRAMMAR
to the station	istasyona	ees-tas-yo-na
toast	kızarmış ekmek	kuh-zar-muhsh ek-mek
tobacconist's	tekel bayii	te-kel ba-yee-ee
today	bugün	boo-gewn

together	beraber	be-ra-ber
toilet	tuvalet	too-va-let
toilet paper	tuvalet kağıdı	too-va-let ka-a-duh
there is no toilet paper	tuvalet kağıdı yok	too-va-let ka-a-u-duh yok
token	jeton	zhe-ton
toll (on motorway, etc.)	geçiş ücreti	ge-cheesh ewdj-re-tee
tomato	domates	do-ma-tes
tomato juice	domates suyu	do-ma-tes soo-yoo
tomato salad	domates salatası	do-ma-tes sa-la-ta-suh
tomorrow	yarın	ya-ruhn
tomorrow morning	yarın sabah	ya-ruhn sa-bah
tomorrow evening	yarın akşam	ya-ruhn ak-sham
tonight	bu akşam	boo ak-sham
tooth	diş	deesh
toothache	diş ağrısı	deesh a-ruh-suh
toothbrush	diş fırçası	deesh fuhr-cha-suh
toothpaste	diş macunu	deesh ma-djoo-noo
torch (electric)	el feneri	el fe-ne-ree
total	toplam	top-lam
tough (meat)	sert	sert
tour	tur	toor
tourist	turist	too-reest
tourist office	turizm bürosu	too-ree-zeem bew-ro-soo
towel	havlu	hav-loo
tower	kule	koo-le
town	şehir	she-heer
town hall	belediye binası	be-le-dee-ye bee-na-suh
toy	oyuncak	o-yoon-djak
traditional	geleneksel	ge-le-nek-sel
traffic	trafik	tra-feek

traffic lights	trafik ışıkları	tra-feek uh-shuk-la-ruh
train	tren	tren
trainers (shoes)	spor ayakkabısı	spor a-yak-ka-buh-suh
to translate	tercüme etmek	ter-djew-me et-mek
to travel	seyahat etmek	se-ya-hat et-mek
travel agent	seyahat acentası	se-ya-hat a-djen-ta-suh
travellers' cheques	seyahat çeki	se-ya-hat che-kee
tree	ağaç	a-ach
trip: *a day trip*	günübirlik gezi	gew-new-beer-leek ge-zee
trousers	pantolon	pan-to-lon
trout	alabalık	a-la-ba-luhk
truck	kamyon	kam-yon
true: *that's true*	doğru	do-roo
that's not true	doğru değil	do-roo de-eel
trunks (swimming)	erkek mayosu	er-kek ma-yo-soo
try on: *can I try it on?*	deneyebilir miyim?	de-ne-ye-bee-leer mee-yeem?
T-shirt	tişört	tee-shurt
Tuesday	Salı	sa-luh
tuna	ton balığı	ton ba-luh-uh
tunnel	tünel	tew-nel
turkey	hindi	heen-dee
Turkey	Türkiye	tewr-kee-ye
Turkish (language)	Türkçe	tewrk-che
Turkish bath	hamam	ha-mam
to turn off (radio, light)	kapamak	ka-pa-mak
to turn on	açmak	ach-mak
tweezers	cımbız	djuhm-buhz
twins	ikizler	ee-keez-ler

U

ugly	çirkin	cheer-keen
umbrella	şemsiye	shem-see-ye
uncle (paternal)	amca	am-dja
(maternal)	dayı	da-yuh
uncomfortable	rahatsız	ra-hat-suhz
underground (metro)	metro	met-ro
understand	anlamak	an-la-mak
I don't understand	anlamıyorum	an-la-muh-yo-room
do you understand?	anlıyor musun?	an-luh-yor moo-soon?
underwear	iç çamaşırı	eech cha-ma-shuh-ruh
unemployed	işsiz	eesh-seez
unleaded petrol	kurşunsuz benzin	koor-shoon-sooz ben-zeen
university	üniversite	ew-nee-ver-see-te
unlucky	şanssız	shans-suhz
upstairs	üstkat	ewst-kat
urgent: it's urgent	acildir	a-djeel-deer
to use	kullanmak	kool-lan-mak
useful	faydalı	fay-da-luh
usually	genellikle	ge-nel-leek-le

V

vacancy (room)	boş oda	bosh o-da
vacuum cleaner	elektrik süpürgesi	e-lek-treek sew-pewr-ge-see
valid	geçerli	ge-cher-lee
valuables	kıymetli eşya	kuhy-met-lee esh-ya
van	kamyonet	kam-yo-net
VAT	KDV	ka-de-ve
veal	dana eti	da-na e-tee
vegetable	sebze	seb-ze

213

vegetarian	vejetaryen	vee-zhe-tar-yen
very	çok	chok
very good	çok iyi	chok ee-yee
view	manzara	man-za-ra
village	köy	khuy
vineyard	üzüm bağı	ew-zewm ba-uh
visa	vize	vee-ze
to visit	ziyaret etmek	zee-ya-ret et-mek
visitor	ziyaretçi	zee-ya-ret-chee
vitamin pills	vitamin hapları	vee-ta-meen hap-la-ruh
volleyball	voleybol	vo-ley-bol
voltage	voltaj	vol-tazh
what is the voltage?	kaç voltaj?	kach vol-tazh?

W

to wait (for)	beklemek	bek-le-mek
please wait	lütfen bekleyin	lewt-fen bek-le-yeen
waiter/waitress	garson	gar-son
waiting room	bekleme odası	bek-le-me o-da-suh
to wake up	uyanmak	oo-yan-mak
Wales	Galler	gal-ler
I'm from Wales	Gallerdenim	gal-ler-de- neem
to walk	yürümek	yew-rew-mek
walk (activity)	yürüyüş	yew-rew-yewsh
(route)	yürüme yeri	yew-rew-me ye-ree
walking-stick	baston	bas-ton
wallet	cüzdan	djewz-dan
walnut	ceviz	ce-veez
to want	istemek	ees-te-mek
war	savaş	sa-vash
wardrobe	gardrop	gar-duh-rop
warm	ılık	uh-luhk
to wash	yıkamak	yuh-ka-mak

washbasin	lavabo	la-va-bo
washing machine	çamaşır makinası	cha-ma-shur ma-kee-na-suh
washing powder	çamaşır deterjanı	cha-ma-shur de-ter-zha-nuh
wasp	yaban arısı	ya-ban a-ruh-suh
watch (wrist)	kol saati	kol sa-a-tee
water	su	soo
distilled water	damıtılmış su	da-muh-tuhl-mush soo
fresh water	tatlı su	tat-luh soo
mineral water	maden suyu	ma-den soo-yoo
waterfall	çağlayan; şelâle	chah-la-yan; she-la-le
waterproof	su geçirmez	soo ge-cheer-mez
water-skiing	su kayağı	soo ka-ya-uh
wave	dalga	dal-ga
way: *is this the right way?*	bu doğru yol mu?	boo do-roo yol muh?
way out	çıkış	chuh-kuhsh
we	biz	beez
weak (tea, coffee, drink)	açık	a-chuk
to wear	giymek	geey-mek
weather forecast	hava durumu	ha-va doo-roo-moo
wedding	evlilik; düğün	ev-lee-lek; dew-ewn
wedding ring	alyans	al-yans
Wednesday	Çarşamba	char-sham-ba
week	hafta	haf-ta
next week	gelecek hafta	ge-le-djek haf-ta
last week	geçen hafta	ge-chen haf-ta
weekend	hafta sonu	haf-ta so-noo
weekly	haftalık	haf-ta-luhk
weight	ağırlık	a-uhr-luhk
welcome!	hoşgeldiniz!	hosh-gel-dee-neez!
well	iyi	ee-yee
well done (meat)	iyi pişmiş	ee-yee peesh-meesh

215

west	batı	ba-tuh
wet	ıslak	uhs-lak
wetsuit	dalgıç elbisesi	dal-guhch el-bee-se-see
what	ne?	ne?
what is it?	bu nedir?	boo ne-deer?
wheelchair	tekerlekli sandalye	te-ker-lek-lee san-dal-ye
when?	ne zaman?	ne za-man?
where?	nerede?	ne-re-de?
which?	hangi?	han-gee?
which one?	hangisi?	han-gee-see?
white	beyaz	be-yaz
who	kim	keem
whole	tüm; bütün; tam	tewm; bew-tewn; tam
whose: *whose is it?*	kimin?	kee-meen?
why	neden	ne-den
wife	eş; hanım	esh; ha-nuhm
window (house)	pencere	pen-jeh-reh
(shop)	vitrin	veet-reen
windsurfing	rüzgar sörfü	rewz-gar sur-few
windy: *it's windy*	rüzgarlı	rewz-gar-luh
wine	şarap	sha-rap
red wine	kırmızı şarap	kuhr-muh-zuh sha-rap
white wine	beyaz şarap	be-yaz sha-rap
wine list	şarap listesi	sha-rap lees-te-see
the wine list, please	şarap listesi, lütfen	sha-rap lees-te-see, lewt-fen
winter	kış	kuhsh
with	ile	ee-le
without	-siz/-sız	see GRAMMAR
woman	kadın	ka-duhn
wood (substance)	tahta	tah-ta
word	kelime	ke-lee-me

to work	çalışmak	cha-luhsh-mak
it doesn't work	çalışmıyor	cha-luhsh-muh-yor
wrap: *please wrap it up*	lütfen paketleyin	lewt-fen pa-ket-le-yeen
to write	yazmak	yaz-mak
writing paper	yazı kağıdı	ya-zuh ka-uh-duh
wrong	yanlış	yan-luhsh

X

x-ray	röntgen	rurnt-gen

Y

yacht	yat	yat
year	yıl	yuhl
this year	bu yıl	boo yuhl
yellow	sarı	sa-ruh
yes	evet	e-vet
yesterday	dün	dewn
you	siz; sen	seez; sen
youth hostel	gençlik yurdu	gench-leek yoor-doo

Z

zero	sıfır	suh-fuhr
zip	fermuar	fer-moo-ar
zoo	hayvanat bahçesi	hay-va-nat bah-che-see

Aa

AB	EU
acenta	agent
acı	pain; bitter
acil	urgent
acil çıkış	emergency exit
acil servis	emergency; A&E
açık	open; light *(colour)*; weak *(tea)*
açmak	to turn on; to open
ad	name
ada	island
adam	man
ağaç	tree
ağrı	pain; ache
ağrıkesici	painkiller
Ağustos	August
ahşap	wooden
ahtapot	octopus
aile	family
Akdeniz	Mediterranean
akşam	evening
akşam yemeği	dinner; evening meal
aktarma	connection *(train, flight)*
alabalık	trout
alışveriş	shopping
alışveriş merkezi	shopping centre
alkolsüz	non-alcoholic
Almanca	German *(language)*
Almanya	Germany
ambulans	ambulance
amca	uncle *(paternal)*
anahtar	key; switch
ananas	pineapple
ançuvez	anchovies
anıt	monument

anne	mother
antika eşya	antiques
araba	car; trolley
araba yıkama	car wash
araç giremez	no entry for vehicles
Aralık	December
aramak	to look for
arı	bee
arkadaş	friend
armut	pears
asansör	lift (*elevator*)
asgari hız	minimum speed
askeri bölge	military zone
at	horse
ateş	fire; heat; fever
Avrupa	Europe
avukat	lawyer
ay	month; moon
ayak	foot
ayakkabı	shoe
ayakkabı bağı	shoe laces
ayna	mirror
ayran	drink made of yoghurt
az	few; little
azami	maximum

Bb

baba	father
badem	almonds
bagaj	luggage; baggage
baharatlı	spicy
bahçe	garden
bahşiş	tip (*to waiter, etc*)
bal	honey
balayı	honeymoon

balık	fish
balıkçı	fishmonger's
banka	bank
banyo	bathroom
banyo havlusu	bath towel
bardak	drinking glass
baş ağrısı	headache
başkonsolosluk	general consulate
batı	west
bavul	suitcase
Bay	Mr
Bayan	Miss; Mrs; Ms
bayanlar tuvaleti	ladies' toilet
bayat	old; stale
bayrak	flag
bebek	baby; doll
bebek bakıcısı	baby-sitter
bebek karyolası	cot
bebek maması	baby food
bedava	free of charge
beden	size *(clothes)*; body; trunk
bekar	single *(unmarried)*
bekleme odası	waiting room
belediye	municipality
belge	document; certificate
ben	I
benzin	petrol
benzin istasyonu	petrol station
berber	barber
beyaz	white
beyin	brain
bıçak	knife
biftek	steak
bilet	ticket
bilet satış	ticket office

bilgi	information
bilgisayar	computer
bilmek	to know
binmek	to get on *(vehicle)*; to ride *(horse)*
bira	beer *(lager)*
biraz	some
bisiklet	bicycle
bitti	finished, sold out
bonfile	fillet steak
borcu olmak	to owe
boş	empty; unoccupied
boş oda	vacancies
bot	boat
boyun	neck
bozuk	broken; out of order
böbrek	kidney
böcek	insect
börek	Turkish pie
broşür	brochure
bu	this; this one
bugün	today
bulaşık makinası	dishwasher
burun	nose
buz	ice
buzdolabı	fridge
buzlu	iced; with ice
buzlu çay	iced tea
buzluk	cool box *(for picnics)*
buzlu kahve	iced coffee
büro	office
büyük	big
büyükelçilik	embassy

Cc

cadde (cad.)	street
cami	mosque
cankurtaran	lifeguard
cankurtaran botu	lifeboat
cankurtaran yeleği	life jacket
ceket	jacket
cevap	answer
ceviz	walnut
ceza	fine *(penalty)*
cibinlik	mosquito net
ciddi	serious
ciğer	liver
ciklet	chewing-gum
cips	crisps
Cuma	Friday
Cumartesi	Saturday
cüzdan	wallet

Çç

çabuk	quick
çadır	tent
çağlayan	waterfall
çalmak	to ring *(bell)*; to play *(instrument)*; to steal *(money)*
çamaşır	laundry
çamaşır deterjanı	washing powder
çamaşır makinası	washing machine
çamaşırhane	launderette
çam fıstığı	pine nuts
çanta	bag
Çarşamba	Wednesday
çarşı	shopping area
çatal	fork *(for eating)*

çay	tea
çek	cheque
çekici	attractive *(person)*
çekiniz	pull
çekmek	to pull
çeşme	fountain
çeviri	translation
çiçek	flowers
çıkış	exit
çıkmak	to go out; to get out
çift	couple *(two people)*
çiftçi	farmer
çift kişilik oda	double room
çiftlik	farm
çikolata	chocolate
çilek	strawberry
çimen	grass
çizgi film	cartoons
çizme	boots
çocuk	child
çok	very; many
çorap	socks
çorba	soup
çöp	litter
çürük	rotten *(food)*

Dd

dağ	mountain
dahil	included
dakika	minute
dalmak	to dive
dana eti	veal
danışma	information
dantel	lace *(material)*
dar	narrow

davet	invitation
davet etmek	to invite
davetiye	invitation
değerli	valuable
değil	not *(it is not...)*
deniz	sea
denizanası	jellyfish
deniz gözlüğü	goggles *(for swimming)*
deprem	earthquake
derece	temperature
deri	leather; skin
deve	camel
dış	external; foreign
dış hatlar	international flights
dikkat	attention
dikkat ediniz!	be careful!
dil	tongue; language
dilim	slice
dinlemek	to listen to
dinlenmek	to rest
diş	tooth
diş fırçası	toothbrush
diş hekimi	dentist
diş macunu	toothpaste
dişçi	dentist
diz	knee
doğu	east
doğum günü	birthday
doğum tarihi	date of birth
doktor	doctor
dokunmayınız	do not touch
dolap	cupboard; wardrobe; locker; fridge
doldurmak	to fill up
dolgu	filling *(for tooth)*

dolmuş	shared minibus
dolu	full; engaged; occupied
domates	tomato
dondurma	ice cream
donmuş	frozen
dönmek	to return
dönüş	return
gidiş-dönüş bilet	return ticket
döviz	foreign currency
döviz bürosu	bureau de change
döviz kuru	exchange rate
duble	double
duman	smoke
dur	stop *(road sign)*
durmak yasak	no stopping
duş	shower *(bath)*
duş bonesi	shower cap
duymak	to hear
dün	yesterday
düşmek	to fall
düşünmek	to think
düz	straight on; flat
düzine	dozen

Ee

eczane	chemist's
Ege Denizi	Aegean Sea
ehliyet	driving licence
Ekim	October
ekmek	bread
el	hand
el bagajı	hand luggage
elbise	dress
eldiven	gloves
elektrikçi	electrician

el havlusu	hand towel
elma	apples
elma çayı	apple tea
elmas	diamond
el yapımı	hand-made
emanet bürosu	left-luggage office
emekli	retired; pensioner; senior citizen
emlakçı	estate agent
emniyet kemeri	seat belt
enformasyon	information
engelli	disabled
erik	plums
erkek	man; male
erkek arkadaş	boyfriend; male friend
erkek kardeş	brother
erkek tuvaleti	gents' toilet
eski	old *(goods)*
eş	husband; wife; partner
et	meat
etli	with meat
etek	skirt
ev	house; home
evet	yes
evli	married
Eylül	September

Ff

fabrika	factory
fakir	poor *(not rich)*
fare	mouse
farklı	different
fatura	invoice
feribot	car ferry
fındık	hazelnut
fırın	oven; baker's

fırtına	storm
fıstık	pistachio
fiks menü	set menu
fiş	plug *(electrical)*; receipt
fiyat listesi	price list
fotoğraf çekmek yasak	photography prohibited
fotokopi	photocopy
Fransızca	French *(language)*
frigo	ice lolly

Gg

garson	waiter; waitress
gazete	newspaper
gece	night; at night
gece yarısı	midnight
gecikme	delay
geç	late
geçerli	valid
gelecek	next
geleneksel	traditional
geliş	arrivals
genç	young
gerçek	real; genuine
geri	back
geri dönmek	to go back; to return
getirmek	to bring; to fetch
gezi	trip
gidiş	departure; single *(ticket)*
gidiş-dönüş	round trip
giriş	entrance; entry
giriş ücreti	entrance fee
giriş yapmak	to check in
girmek	to go in; to get into; to enter
gişe	box office; ticket office
giymek	to wear

göbek dansı	belly dancing
göğüs	chest (of body)
gökyüzü	sky
göl	lake
görmek	to see
göstermek	to show
göz	eye
göz doktoru	ophthalmologist
gözlük	glasses (spectacles)
greyfurt	grapefruit
gri	grey
gül	rose
gümrük	customs
gümrük kontrol	customs control
gümüş	silver
gün	day
günaydın	good morning
güneş	sun
güneş çarpması	sunstroke
güneş gözlüğü	sunglasses
güneş kremi	suntan lotion
güneşli	sunny
güneşlik	sunshade
güneş yanığı	sunburn
güney	south
günlük	diary
gürültülü	noisy
güzel	beautiful; fine

Hh

haberler	news
hafta	week
hafta içi	weekday
hafta sonu	weekend
halı	carpet (rug)

hamam	Turkish baths
harabe	ruin
hardal	mustard
harita	map
hasta	ill
hastalık	disease
hastane (hst.)	hospital
haşlama	boiled
hatıra	souvenir
hatırlamak	to remember
havaalanı	airport
havayolu	airline
havlu	towel
havuz	pool
hayır	no
hayvanat bahçesi	zoo
Haziran	June
hediye	present *(gift)*
hediyelik eşya dükkanı	gift shop; souvenir shop
hemen	immediately
hemşire	nurse
hepsi	all
her	every
her zaman	always
hesap	bill; account
Hıristiyan	Christian
hırsız	thief
hız	speed
hız sınırı	speed limit
hız sınırı sonu	end of speed restriction
hızlı	fast
hiç	none; no
hindi	turkey *(bird)*
hindistan cevizi	coconut
hizmet	service

I i

hizmetçi	maid
hostes	stewardess
hoş	pretty; nice
hoşçakal	goodbye
hoşbulduk!	response to welcome
hoşlanmak	to enjoy; to like
hurma	dates *(fruit)*

Iı

ılık	warm
ısı	heat; temperature
ısırık	bite; sting
ısıtıcı	heater
ıslak	wet
ıstakoz	lobster
ızgara	grilled; grill
ızgara köfte	small grilled meatballs

İi

iadeli taahhütlü mektup	registered letter
içecek	drink
iç hatlar	domestic flights
içilmez	not for drinking
içme suyu	drinking water
ikametgâh adresi	place of residence
ikaz üçgeni	warning triangle
ikinci kat	second floor
ikiz	twins
ilaç	medicine *(drug)*
ilginç	interesting
ilk yardım	first aid
ilkbahar	spring *(season)*
ilkbaharda	in spring
imdat!	help!

imdat freni	emergency stop cord *(train)*
imkansız	impossible
imza	signature
inci	pearl
incir	fig
indirim	discount
indirimli satışlar	sale
inek eti	beef
İngiliz	English; British
İngiliz anahtarı	spanner
İngilizce	English *(language)*
İngiltere	England; Britain
İngiltere Konsolosluğu	British Consulate
İngiltere Büyükelçiliği	British Embassy
iniş	landing *(airplane)*
inmek	to go down; to get off; to land
ipek	silk
iptal etmek	to cancel
isim	name
istasyon	station
istemek	to want
istiridye	oyster
iş	job; work
itfaiye	fire brigade
itmek	to push
iyi	well; good
iyi akşamlar	good evening
iyi geceler	goodnight
iyi pişmiş	well done *(meat)*
izin	permit

Jj

jambon	ham
jeton	token *(for boat, phone etc)*
jilet	razor blade

jimnastik ayakkabısı	gym shoes; trainers
jöle	jelly

Kk

kabuklu deniz ürünleri	shellfish
kabul etmek	to accept
kaç?	how many?
kaç lira?	how much? *(price)*
kaç tane?	how many?
kaçırmak	to miss *(plane, train, etc)*
kadın	woman
kadınlar tuvaleti	ladies' toilet
kahvaltı	breakfast
kahve	coffee
kahverengi	brown
kakao	cocoa
kalamar	squid
kale	castle
kalite	quality
kalkış	departure
kalp	heart
kamp yapmak	to camp
kamp yapmak yasaktır	no camping
kamp yeri	campsite
kamyon	lorry
kan	blood
kapalı	closed, switched off
kapatmak	to close; to switch off
kapı	gate *(at airport)*; door
kapıyı kapatın	close the door
kar	snow
kara	black
karabiber	black pepper
Karadeniz	Black Sea
kardeş (erkek)	brother

kardeş (kız)	sister
karıncalar	ants
karışık	mixed
kart	postcard; card *(greetings)*
kas	muscle
kasa	cash desk; safe
kasap	butcher's
Kasım	November
kaşık	spoon
kavanoz	jar
kavşak	junction
kayak	skiing; ski
kayınpeder	father-in-law
kayınvalide	mother-in-law
kayıp	lost; missing *(thing)*
kayıp eşya bürosu	lost property
kayıt ücreti	registration charge
kaymaklı	creamy
kaynamış	boiled *(food)*
kaz	goose
kaza	accident
KDV	VAT
kedi	cat
kemer	belt
kertenkele	lizard
kestane	chestnuts
kestirme	short cut
keten	linen
kılıç balığı	swordfish
kırık	fractured; broken
kırmızı	red
kırmızı şarap	red wine
kırtasiye	stationer's
kısa	short
kış	winter

kıyma	minced meat
kıymetli eşya	valuables
kız	girl
kızamık	measles
kız arkadaş	girlfriend; female friend
kızarmış	fried *(food)*
kızarmış ekmek	toast
kızarmış patates	fried potatoes; chips
kızartma	fried
kız evlat	daughter
kızgın	angry
kız kardeş	sister
kızlık soyadı	maiden name
kibrit	matches *(light)*
kilim	rug
kilise	church
kilitlemek	to lock
kilitli dolap	locker *(for luggage)*
kim?	who?
kimlik	identification
kiralık	to rent; for hire
kiralık oda	rooms to let
kiraz	cherries
kirli	dirty
kitap	book
kişi	person
kişniş otu	coriander
klima	air conditioning
koklamak	to smell
koku	smell
kol	arm
Kola	Coke®
kolay	easy
koli	parcel
koltuk	seat

kompartıman	compartment *(on train)*
komşu	neighbour
konserve açacağı	tin-opener
kontak lens	contact lens
kontak lens temizleyici	contact lens cleaner
kova	bucket
koyu	dark; strong *(tea, coffee)*
koyun	sheep
koyun eti	mutton
köfte	meatball
köpek	dog
köprü	bridge *(road, etc)*; crown *(on tooth)*
köpüklü	sparkling; fizzy
köpüksüz	still *(not fizzy)*
kör	blind *(person)*
köşe	corner
kötü	bad; evil
köy	village
kraliçe	queen
kravat	tie
krem	cream *(cosmetic)*
krema	cream *(dairy)*
krep	pancake, crépe
kuaför	hairdresser
kuduz	rabies
kulak	ear
kule	tower
kulüp	club *(sports, social)*
kum	sand
kur	rate
kurallar	regulations
Kurban Bayramı	Feast of Sacrifice *(Muslim feast)*
kurşunsuz benzin	unleaded petrol
kuru	dry; dried

kuru temizleyeci	dry-cleaner's
kurutmak	to dry
kuru üzüm	sultana
kuş	bird
kuşkonmaz	asparagus
kuşüzümü	currant
kutu	box
kuyruk	queue; tail
kuyumcu	jeweller's
kuzey	north
kuzu	lamb
küçük	little; small
külotlu çorap	tights
kül tablası	ashtray

Ll

lacivert	navy blue
leziz	delicious
liman	harbour
limonata	lemon drink
Lira	Turkish currency
lokanta	restaurant
lokum	Turkish delight
losyon	lotion
lüks	luxurious
lütfen	please

Mm

maç	match *(game)*
maden suyu	mineral water
mağara	cave
makarna	pasta
makas	scissors
manastır	monastery

manav	greengrocer's; fruit shop
mantar	mushrooms; cork
manzara	view
margarin	margarine
marmelat	marmalade
Mart	March
masa	table
masa tenisi	table tennis
mavi	blue
Mayıs	May
mayo	swimsuit
mektup	letter *(mail)*
mercek	lens *(for camera)*
merdiven	stairs
merhaba	hello
merkez	centre
mermer	marble
mesai saatleri	opening hours
mesaj	message
meşrubat	soft drink
meyve	fruit
meyve suyu	fruit juice
mezarlık	cemetery
meze	appetizers
mide	stomach
midye	mussels
mikrodalga	microwave *(oven)*
milliyet	nationality
mimar	architect
misafir	guest
misafirhane	guest-house
mobilya	furniture
moda	fashion
motorsiklet	motorbike
muhallebici	sweets and desserts shop

mum	candle
muslukçu	plumber
mutfak	kitchen
mutlu	happy
muz	banana
mücevher	jewellery
müdür	manager
müdüriyet	management
mükemmel	excellent; perfect
müracaat	enquiry desk
Müslüman	Muslim
müze	museum

Nn

nakit	cash
nane	mint
nar	pomegranate
nasıl?	how?
naylon poşet	plastic bag
ne?	what?
neden?	why?
nefes almak	to breathe
nehir	river
nektarin	nectarine
nemlendirici	moisturizer
nerede?	where?
Nescafé®	instant coffee
ne zaman?	when?
nezle	flu
Nisan	April
nişanlı	fiancé(e)
Noel	Christmas
nöbetci	on duty; guard
numara	number

Oo

o	he; she; it
Ocak	January
oda	room *(of house, etc)*
oda servisi	room service
ofis	office
okul	school
olgun	ripe *(fruit, vegetable)*, mature *(person)*
olta	fishing-rod
olta yemi	bait *(for fishing)*
omlet	omelette
onlar	they
opera	opera
operatör	operator *(telephone)*
orada	there
ordövr	hors d'œuvre
orman	forest
orta	medium; medium-sweet *(coffee)*
ortak	partner *(business)*
orta pişmiş	medium rare *(meat)*
otel	hotel
otobüs	coach; bus
otobüs durağı	bus stop
otobüs terminali	bus station
otobüs turu	bus tour
otobüs yolculuğu	coach trip
otogar	coach station
otomatik	automatic
otopark	car park
otoyol	motorway
oturma odası	living room
oyun	play; performance; game
oyuncak	toy

Öö

ödünç vermek	to lend
öğleden sonra	afternoon; in the afternoon
öğle yemeği	lunch
öğrenci	student
öğretmen	teacher; instructor
ön	front
önce	before; ago
önemli	important
öpmek	to kiss
ördek	duck *(meat)*
özel	private; special
özel banyo	private bathroom
özel fiyat	special price

Pp

pahalı	expensive
paket	packet
palto	coat
pamuk	cotton
pancar	beetroot
pansiyon	guest house, B&B
pantolon	trousers
papaz	priest
para	money
pardon	pardon; excuse me
park	park
parti	party *(celebration)*
pasaport	passport
pasaport kontrolü	passport control
pasta	pastry *(cake)*
pastane	cake shop; pâtisserie
patates	potato
paten	skates

paylaşmak	to share
Pazar	Sunday
pazar	bazaar, farmers' market
pazarlık	to bargain
Pazartesi	Monday
peçete	napkin
pembe	pink
peron	platform *(railway)*
Perşembe	Thursday
peynir	cheese
peynirli	with cheese
peynirli börek	cheese pastry
peynirli omlet	cheese omelette
pırasa	leeks
pide	pitta bread
pijama	pyjamas
pil	battery *(for torch, radio, etc)*
pilav	pilau rice; boiled rice
pipo	pipe *(for smoking)*
pire	fleas
pirzola	cutlet; chop
plaj	beach
plaj havlusu	beach towel
plaka	number plate
polis	police officer
pompa	pump *(for tyres)*
portakal	orange
portakal reçeli	marmelade
portakal suyu	orange juice
posta	post
posta kartı	postcard
posta kodu	postcode
posta kutusu	postbox; letterbox
postane	post office
poşet çay	tea bag

prezervatif	condoms
priz	socket *(electric)*
protez	dentures
PTT	post office
pul	stamp
puro	cigar
püre	mashed potato

Rr

radyo	radio
raf	shelf
rahat	comfortable
rahatsız	uncomfortable
raket	racquet
rakı	aniseed drink *(alcoholic)*
Ramazan	Ramadan *(Muslim month of fasting)*
randevu	appointment
rapor	report
reçel	jam *(food)*
reçete	prescription
rehber	guidebook; guide
rehberli tur	guided tour
reklam	advertisement
renk	colour
resepsiyon	reception *(desk)*
resim	picture *(on wall)*
resmi	official
resmi tatil	public holiday
rezervasyon	reservation
rezervasyon bürosu	booking office
rezerve etmek	to reserve *(room, table, etc)*
rıhtım	quay
röntgen	x-ray
ruj	lipstick

rüzgar	wind
rüzgar sörfü	windsurfing

Ss

saat (sa.)	hour; clock
saat kaç?	what time is it?
sabah	morning
sabun	soap
saç	hair
saç fırçası	hairbrush
saç kestirmek	haircut
saç kremi	conditioner *(for hair)*
saç kurutma makinası	hair dryer
sade	simple; plain; unsweetened
sade pilav	plain boiled rice
sadece	only
sağ	right
sağda	on/to the right
sağır	deaf
sahanda yumurta	fried eggs
sahil	coast
sahil güvenlik	coastguard
sahip	owner
sakin	quiet
salata	salad
salatalık	cucumber
salça	tomato paste
Salı	Tuesday
salon	lounge
saman nezlesi	hay fever
sanat	art
sanatçı	artist
sanat galerisi	art gallery
sandal	sandals; rowing boat; dinghy
sandalye	chair *(seat)*

sandviç	sandwich
saray	palace
sardalye	sardines
sarhoş	drunk
sarı	yellow
sarılık	hepatitis; jaundice
sarımsak	garlic
sarışın	blonde
satılık	for sale
satmak	to sell
savaş	war
sebze	vegetables
sel	flood
sen	you
sepet	basket
sergi	exhibition; display
sert	tough; hard
sertifika	certificate
servis ücreti	service charge
sevimli	attractive
seyahat	to travel
seyahat acentası	travel agent
seyahat çeki	travellers' cheques
sıcak	hot
sıfır	zero
sığır	cattle
sığır eti	beef
sıkıcı	boring
sık sık	often; frequent
sınır	border (of country); limit
sırt çantası	rucksack; backpack
sızıntı	leak
sigara	cigarettes
sigara içilir	smoking
sigara içilmez	non-smoking

sigorta	insurance; fuse
sirk	circus
sis	fog
sivrisinek	mosquito
siyah	black
siz	you
soğan	onion
soğuk	cold
sokak (sok.)	street
sol	left
solda/sola	on/to the left
somon	salmon
son	last; end
sonbahar	autumn
sonra	after
soru	question
sos	sauce
sosis	sausage
soyadı	surname
sörf tahtası	surfboard
sörf yapmak	to surf
sözlük	dictionary
spor	sport
stadyum	stadium
su	water; juice
su kayağı	water-skiing
su sporları	water sports
sucuk	spicy Turkish sausage
suçiçeği	chickenpox
su toplaması	blister
süet	suede
sünger	sponge *(for cleaning)*
sürahi	jug
sürücü	driver
süt	milk

sütlü	with milk
sütlü çikolata	milk chocolate
sütlü kahve	white coffee
sütyen	bra
süveter	sweater

Şş

şaka	joke
şampanya	champagne
şampuan	shampoo
şans	luck
şanssız	unlucky
şanslı	lucky
şapka	hat
şarap	wine
beyaz şarap	white wine
kırmızı şarap	red wine
köpüklü şarap	sparkling wine
şarap listesi	wine list
şarkı	song
şarküteri	delicatessen
şehir	town; city
şehiriçi	local
şehir merkezi	town/city centre
şehir planı	town plan
şeker	sugar; sweets
şekerli	with sugar
şemsiye	umbrella
şerefe!	cheers!
şeri	sherry
şezlong	deck chair
şifalı otlar	herbs
şikayet	complaint
şimdi	now
şirket	company *(business)*

şişe	bottle
şişe açacağı	bottle-opener
şişman	fat
şişmiş	swollen *(finger, ankle, etc)*
şofben	water heater
şort	shorts
Şubat	February

Tt

taahhütlü mektup	registered letter
tabak	plate
tablo	picture; painting
tahta	wood *(substance)*
taklit	fake
takma diş	dentures
taksi	taxi
takvim	calendar
talk pudrası	talcum powder
tam	whole; full
tam pansiyon	full board
tamam	OK; all right
tamir	repair
tamirhane	repair shop
tarife	timetable; tariff
tarih	date *(calendar)*
tat	flavour; taste
tatil	holiday
tatlı	dessert; sweet
tatlı su	fresh water
tava	frying pan; fried
tavşan	rabbit
tavuk	chicken
taze	fresh; young
tebrikler!	congratulations!
tehlike	danger

tek	single *(ticket, item)*
tekel bayi	tobacconist's
tekerlekli sandalye	wheelchair
tek kişilik oda	single room
tekne	boat
tekne gezisi	cruise
tekrar	again
tekrar etmek	to repeat
tek yön	one-way *(street)*
telaffuz etmek	to pronounce
telefon	phone
telefon etmek	to telephone
telefon kartı	phonecard
telefon kodu	dialling code
telefon numarası	phone number
telefon rehberi	telephone directory
telesekreter	answering machine
televizyon	television
telgraf	telegram
temiz	clean
Temmuz	July
tenis	tennis
tenis oynamak	to play tennis
tenis raketi	tennis racquet
tenis topu	tennis ball
tercih etmek	to prefer
tercüman	interpreter
tercüme etmek	to translate
tereyağı	butter
termometre	thermometer
termos	flask
teşekkür ederim	thank you
teşekkürler	thanks
tetanoz	tetanus
teyze	aunt *(maternal)*

tezgâhtar	shop assistant
tıkaç	plug *(for sink)*
tıkandı	blocked
tıraş	shaving
tıraş bıçağı	razor blades
tıraş kremi	shaving cream
tıraş makinası	shaver
tıraş olmak	to shave
tırnak	nail *(finger, toe)*
tişört	t-shirt
tiyatro	theatre
TL	Turkish lira
ton balığı	tuna
tonik	tonic water
top	ball
toplam	total
toplantı	meeting
tost	toasted sandwich, toastie
trafik	traffic
trafik ışıkları	traffic lights
tren	train
tren garı	train station
tren istasyonu	railway station
tur	tour
turist	tourist
turist bileti	tourist ticket
turizm bürosu	tourist office
turp	radish
turşu	pickles
turta	tart; pie
turuncu	orange *(colour)*
tuvalet	toilet
tuvalet kağıdı	toilet paper
tuz	salt
tükenmez kalem	ballpoint pen

tünel	tunnel
Türkçe	Turkish *(language)*
Türkiye	Turkey

Uu

ucuz	cheap
ucuzluk	sale
uçak	airplane
uçuş	flight
uçuş kartı	boarding card
U dönüşü yasak	no U turn
uluslararası	international
uluslararası ehliyet	international driving licence
un	flour
uyku	sleep
uyku ilacı	sleeping pill
uyku tulumu	sleeping bag
uyruk	nationality
uyumak	to sleep
uzak	far
uzun	long; tall
uzunluk	length

Üü

ücret	fare; toll; charge
ülke	country *(not town)*
üst kat	upstairs
üstü kalsın	keep the change
ütü	iron *(for clothes)*
ütülemek	to iron
üye	member *(of club, etc)*
üzgün	sad; sorry
üzüm	grapes

Vv

vadi	valley
valiz	suitcase
vantilatör	fan
vapur	ship; boat; ferry
varış	arrival
varmak	to arrive
vatandaş	citizen
ve	and
vejetaryen	vegetarian
vergi	tax
vermek	to give *(give back)*
veya	or
vezne	cash desk
vida	screw
video	video
viski	whisky
vişne	morello cherries
vitamin hapı	vitamin pills
vize	visa
voleybol	volleyball
votka	vodka

Yy

yabancı	foreigner
yağ	oil
yağmur	rain
yağmurluk	raincoat
yakın	near
yakında	soon; nearby
yakıt	fuel
yangın	fire
yangın alarmı	fire alarm
yangın çıkışı	fire exit

yangın söndürücü	fire-extinguisher
yanlış	mistake
yanmak	to burn
yara bandı	plaster *(for cut)*
yaralı	injured
yardım etmek	to help
yarım	half
yarım pansiyon	half board
yarım saat	half an hour
yarım şişe	half a bottle
yarın	tomorrow
yarış	race *(sport)*
yasak	forbidden
yasak bölge	prohibited area; no entry
yaş	age, wet
yaşamak	to live
yaşlı	old *(person)*
yat	yacht
yatak	bed
yatak odası	bedroom
yavaş	slow
yaya geçidi	pedestrian crossing
yaz	summer
yazmak	to write
yedek	spare
yemek	meal *(food)*
yemek odası	dining room
yemek tarifi	recipe
yemekli vagon	restaurant car
yengeç	crab
yeni	new; recent
Yeni Yıl	New Year
yer	place; space
yerel	local
yerel saat	local time

yerfıstığı	peanuts
yeşil	green
yetişkin	adult
yıkamak	to wash
yıl	year
yılan	snake
yıldız	star
yiyecek	food
yoğurt	yoghurt
yol	road; path; route
yolcu	passenger
yol haritası	road map
yol ver	give way
yumurta	egg
Yunanca	Greek *(language)*
Yunanistan	Greece
yurt	youth hostel; dormitory
yurtdışı	overseas *(postage)*, international
yurtiçi	inland *(postage)*, domestic
yuvarlak	round
yüksek	high; tall
yüksek tansiyon	high blood pressure
yürümek	to walk
yürüyüş	walk
yüz	hundred; face
yüzme havuzu	swimming-pool
yüzmek	to swim
yüzük	ring *(for finger)*
yüzyıl	century

Zz

zaman	time
zarf	envelope
zehir	poison
zehirli	poisonous

zemin	ground
zemin kat	ground floor
zencefil	ginger
zengin	rich
zeytin	olives
zeytinyağı	olive oil
zincir	chain
ziyaret etmek	to visit
ziyaretçi	visitor
zor	difficult